**SAUDADE**
*the possibilities of place*

# saudade

## THE POSSIBILITIES OF PLACE

ANIK SEE

*Coach House Books, Toronto*

Published with the assistance of the Canada Council for the
Arts and the Ontario Arts Council. We also acknowledge
the financial support of the Government of Ontario through
the Ontario Book Publishing Tax Credit Program and
the Government of Canada through the Book Publishing
Industry Development Program.

Canada Council
for the Arts

Conseil des Arts
du Canada

ONTARIO ARTS COUNCIL
CONSEIL DES ARTS DE L'ONTARIO

Canadä

Library and Archives Canada
Cataloguing in Publication

See, Anik
Saudade : the possibilities of place / Anik See.

ISBN 978-1-55245-207-3

1. See, Anik--Travel.  2. Travel.  1. Title.

PS8587.E3466S26 2008    C818'.603    C2008-903533-X

*for Walter and Laszlo*

# Contents •

'And finally, the most important discovery – the people. The locals. How they fit this landscape, this light, these smells. How they are as one with them. How man and environment are bound in an indissoluble, complementary, and harmonious whole. I am struck by how firmly each race is grounded in the terrain in which it lives, in its climate. We shape our landscape, and it, in turn, moulds our physiognomy."

– Ryszard Kapuściński, *The Cobra's Heart*

# Letter to a Friend

# (Whose Mother Is Dying)

Negombo

8 March 2003

C,

THESE ARE MY LAST MOMENTS in Sri Lanka; it just
occurred to me that I haven't written you a letter from here
yet, and that now, of all times (I just received the email
about your mom's seizure), you could probably use one,
if only as solipsistic distraction. I can't know what your
mom's condition will be by the time you receive this; I can
only hope that this letter finds you as well as can be.

I'll set the scene. I'm in a rest house on the 'wrong' (read:
Sri Lankan) side of a resort town, on the beach that accom-
modates the largest fishing setup (too localized to be called
an 'industry,' as there is nothing industrial about it apart
from industriousness of the physical-labour kind) on the
island. Four thousand trawlers and skiffs and outriggers
and other boats (mostly non-motorized) leave from this
beach every day and come back to it with their catch. The
air is pungent. A stand of frangipani trees is scentless against
the fish and partially blocks a view of thatched shacks a
stone's throw away, where some kids are playing cricket,
naked, with a makeshift bat, and one woman is checking
another's hair for lice. A web of homemade electrical wires

provides a patchy canopy. The shacks are between the rest house and the surf, which is fifty feet away. I'm watching some square-sailed outriggers coming into shore ... I've spent an hour watching them already and wish I were on one of them. It's two in the afternoon now and there are about a hundred of them, looking west toward Africa. The fisherfolk are the only ones around today: the entire town is deserted, crowded around someone else's television, because Sri Lanka is playing Australia (largely considered to be the anticipated winner) in the Cricket World Cup. But the fisherfolk don't have electricity and so they might as well work, if only toward a promise of electricity. Even so, it's a country where (present preoccupation with tele-vised cricket matches excepted) television doesn't figure much into a daily routine. Family is paramount. What we have come, in our luxury of psychoanalysis, to call 'qual-ity time' is not part of the vernacular here. It is simply done. Family comes first, in no way that I have ever seen before. In Mexico, family is talked about as being import-ant, but ultimately the spending of time with family there has always struck me as guilt-based (derived from a guilt-oriented religion?) and obligatory. Not unconditional. Here, there is an ease with family that I'm envious of (perhaps derivative of the 'looser' religions here – Buddhism and Hinduism – which spend less time specifically directing their worshippers than asking them to simply embrace religion in whichever way they can, which frees the mind of guilt). Here, the predominant religion is Buddhism. But even in the most sacred Buddhist temples you will see images of, and shrines to, Hindu gods. Vishnu (the protector and preserver), Shiva (the destroyer), Kataragama (god of war) and Ganesh (bringer of prosperity). So, even within Buddhism, there is room for aspects of another religion.

One of the outriggers is in trouble – the top right corner of its sail has come loose from its mast, and I keep hoping that one of the other boats will stop and help, but they just keep sailing past. Sailors may be philosophical, but they are not a particularly helpful lot. Beside me on the stone steps of this quiet courtyard, there is a lame man – the sweeper. He is so thin that the end of his belt comes back around to its buckle. He's trying to feed a puppy the rest of his lunch. He reminds me that we all need something to need us, and maybe that's why we Westerners, who are so independent, mostly fail to understand family in this way, and need to come up with things like 'quality time' to justify such a base need. Everyone here asks if my family is in Sri Lanka, if that's why I've come here. When I say no, they're back in Canada, this confuses them. It's a black mark against me. Why would I leave them? I am a selfish person. (I am.)

Christianity never fit with me. Here it seems important only that you *have* a religion, no matter what kind. And what a place to look for one. Yesterday, a Seventh-day Adventist pastor passing on a motorcycle saw me resting on my bike at a stone wall by a switchback, and he stopped for a chat. When I told him that I knew only one person in Canada who *really* believed in God, he reached into his saddlebag and pulled out a bottle of holy water, doused me in it and said a quick prayer. Then, as I was winding my way through tea plantations, I passed a mountain stream where an offering had been left. Some Tamil/Hindu women washing there told me to leave my own offering among the rice, broken coconuts, cut limes and rose water. I left some fruit, for a safe journey. One of them called me toward her, poured some water over my bent head, sent me on my way. And, finally, toward the end of the day, I passed a roadside shrine where drivers stop to make a quick monetary offering and give a prayer for their own journeys. There was a minivan idling there, and, inside, a Buddhist monk who had opened his window and was doing a quick chant for all of the people in the van. It was a throaty chant and at the end of it, after touching the edges of his palms to his nose and forehead several times, he looked over at me and smiled, laughing. He gave me an enormous pomegranate, said 'Eat!' – held his hands to his forehead again and bowed at me, giving one last chant.

There's a lone man paddling against the surf, trying to get out to the current that will carry him along the same route as the prawns. The prawn fishers here use flat kayaks. Kayaks they sit on, not in – basically just a slab of wood a couple of inches wider than themselves, raised an inch or two above the surface of the water. No more. They go out every night, lolling sideways over the waves, with big, empty baskets set on the slab in front of them. And when they get to where they think the prawns are, they cast a net out, pull it in. The prawns in the net go into the basket. The more this guy catches, the farther away from the basket he'll have to sit so that the boat doesn't start to sink. It's sunset and there he is, heading out, a silhouette sitting on the ocean's surface, diamonds of light coming through his basket, a figure balancing, paddling, casting a net wide like a jellyfish flashing in extension, sometimes standing and scanning the horizon. He'll stay out on the raft all night with only a kerosene lantern and just enough room to stretch his legs out in front of him. If he capsizes in these waves, no one will know. He will simply never come back. Maybe that's what the ocean is: either faith or a ritual of death and renewal. Seventy-five per cent of the earth's surface a prayer.

The outrigger's sail is fixed. The other boats have long since reached shore and are bringing their catch up the beach to makeshift wooden stalls (a 7-Eleven kind of fish market, open twenty-four hours) in big, round wooden baskets that need to be carried by two people. Others are drinking arrack and stretching the nets out to see if they need to be mended. The big trawlers are heading out to sea now, farther than the prawn kayaks, for bigger fish, more fish. When they come in in the morning, the market will be teeming and it will be the best place on the whole island for breakfast and conversation. One guy by the shacks is dry soaping himself in anticipation of the approaching thunderstorm. He's done – he's just standing and waiting now. It's the first rain in three weeks and it's starting, really hard now; the puppy has hidden and is whimpering, and everyone is running inside and laughing. A wall of rain and one guy standing solo in the middle of the street, white with soap lather now. He's laughing too. Or at least I think he is. I can't hear him over the shattering rain. But I can see two bands of white teeth grinning and the red of the inside of his mouth in between. God, how does someone govern her life (or the lives of others) without having seen such things? The man with the belt whose end wraps around to meet its buckle looks at me and we smile. I give him some food and he calls the dog.

What all of this has to do with death and dying, whether past or imminent, I'm not sure. At the very least, it would seem that some comfort might be found in ritual. It's the best thing I can send your way right now, other than good thoughts. I only hope it provides some comfort, no matter how.

(Sadly, but in hope),

A.

IT'S UNCLEAR TO ME whether we're supposed to wait, or to hope.

Spanish is a Romance language, but I didn't realize the small *r* implication of that until someone, a Chilean expat in Tehran, kissed me softly on my cheek and whispered that *hope* and *wait* are expressed using the same word – *esperar* – *en Español*. I was twenty-three at the time, and foolishly chose to presume a personal gravity to his claim instead of merely enjoying the statement itself. I'm thirty now, and not about to reveal this detail to Bill, who shifts uncomfortably on the bench across from me, because he is a lover of the jealous kind, and would take offence to my having even entertained the idea of a man who wasn't him. We are in Holguín, in eastern Cuba, waiting (or hoping) for my luggage to arrive, and it is July, and it is hot. And the woman who I've just spoken to has issued her directive.

*Espero, por favor.*

We wait (and hope) for a day. We accomplish nothing except for perfecting our observational skills. People come to the door of the house where we're staying selling things: 100 heads of garlic for a dollar (no, the heads are too small – in a month they'll be bigger and the same price), coffee, marmalade ... The woman who owns the place holds her hand up in front of her and waves it, up and down, *No, no*. She too hopes, and waits. I've never been one for patience, and her Spanish is better than mine.

We borrow bikes and ride to the ocean, thirty kilometres away. We pedal up and down through lush, rolling land-scape, supersized palms rising from carefully tended fields, Brahman cows – just hide and bones – languorously grazing. Goats bleat and switch their tails and ears in the shade. We ride and ride and the air occasionally crackles with the crow of a rooster. There is no traffic: the roads are marvellously empty. There are no fences or mailboxes – nothing determining possession.

At the end of the road, in Gibara, the sea foams and spews froth, lines of whitecaps like ripples on sand dunes. The white blindness of the light reminds me of the time I spent in a dusty town in northern Argentina, a stone's throw from the Bolivian border. There the houses were long, uninterrupted blocks of fading colonial facades, too, iron grates over doors and windows, barriers to luxuriously simple courtyards. There the conversations were carried out in the middle of the streets, just like they are here, supplemented by shouts from eavesdroppers on balconies above. Words that drift down require more consideration than those projected horizontally. In Gibara, it's hotter than usual, so no one is working, and people have gathered silently in the plaza, staring at the ocean. A baby blue DeSoto drifts past, a couple in wedding dress in the back seat, kissing. The couple's friends follow, crammed into an enclosed truck, a makeshift bus, honking softly. The bride turns away from her new husband for a moment, toward the back window, looks out, catches my eye and smiles. The DeSoto creaks down the street, swaying drunkenly around potholes; watching it is like watching time slow right before your eyes.

We wait, we hope. This morning when I woke, I thought I was in Iran again. A *braaaaahhhhp* of mopeds outside, the muffled honks of pre-revolution cars, the slapping of laundry against stone, a man's coarse skin against mine at dawn. Someone chopping fruit – the sounds of the blade on wood echoing up the walls toward an open ceiling.

*Espero*

Santiago de Cuba is preparing for its infamous annual carnival. Out on the street, ten enormous tankers, each carrying a factory-sized brewing vat of beer, rumble slowly by. They park and set up behind lean-tos made of palm fronds and bamboo. On the main street in town, stages are being erected. Masks are being sold, costumes are being adjusted, hemmed, altered. Musicians walk up and down the streets carrying their instruments, breaking into song at whim. Entire bands congregate in the living rooms of houses; neighbours stand outside the windows and doors, peering in, listening, dancing. In the evening we go to a *Casa de la Trova*, where two Santiagan bands play more *campesino* music, and where the audience gets up and moves slowly at first, then quickly, constantly changing partners, shaking their bodies with vigour and pleasure. The most popular woman there is close to ninety years old, with dyed blonde hair and wrinkles the whole length of her body. She can barely walk from her chair to the band, but when the music starts, she wriggles and grooves her way through the music like she wrote it herself.

Casa de la Trova " Pepe Sánchez "

Comprobante de Entrada No. _____

Fecha: _____

Precio: _____ U.S.D.

001801    VISITANTE

Younger women in skin-tight dresses try to compete, sneaking furtive glances at her when her back is turned and then mimicking her. The men shake and groove and grin and whistle and suck their breath.

At midnight, large papier mâché heads of fairy-tale characters bounce down the *avenida*. The *avenida* bottlenecks, the dancing stops, the heads come off. Children jiggle up and down on the edge, craning to see their favourite character. For twenty minutes they are stopped, then they suddenly start again. African colonial dancers in long white dresses, swaying hips and shoulders. The *avenida* bottlenecks, the dancing stops. Then starts again after ten minutes. Caribbean drummers in baby blue polyesters with black frilled sleeves doing the conga all the way down the street. The *avenida* bottlenecks, the dancing stops. Etc., etc.

In the alleyways, women pluck each other's eyebrows on the crumbling stone steps of their houses. Firecrackers go off, people drag their stereo speakers out into the street, playing *son*, and dance, dance, dance. Bill and I are fighting – he's angry again that I'm not paying enough attention to him, and goes back to our room to sulk – there is nothing I can do, so I dance, too, until dawn, and then I walk back to our room on deserted streets dusted in early morning light, where I catch Bill coming back, too, with a sheepish grin on his face.

A man on a horse (he's even got spurs on) outside a bar offers us a swig of a rough, homemade rum, grins with black teeth and lets out a lovely, soft laugh.

We wake to the sound of sweeping and low chatter. I want to take this sound and carry it home with me, press Play in the middle of a January snowstorm when it's still dark at eight-thirty in the morning. Maria, the sister-in-law of the geologist at whose place we're staying, kisses both of my cheeks every time she sees us. I want to carry that home with me too. She shows me how to make *tostones*, fried slices of plantain on a stove fuelled by a thick, black oil mixture that she scoops out of a drum. Later, she says, her brother will make *chicharrón*, pig skin fried in its own fat. She points to a bowl filled with red and white. Fat and blood, fresh from the pig that has disappeared from the courtyard. The courtyard we woke to her sweeping this morning.

I go for a walk out of town, and every time I pass someone, they shout '*el veinte y seis!*' ('the twenty-sixth!') at me. The day of the revolution. Is today. There are many days of revolution in Cuba. This one is based on failure. I like that only the truly socialist take stock in failure.

Tall thunderheads form tall on the horizon, exploding like yeast in warm water. The rain lets loose and turns the road into immobilizing mud. I duck into a dark, abandoned house on the side of the road. The rain stops after half an hour, but the lightning continues into early evening and I sit in the dirt with chickens, a dog, a cat, a turkey and a pig who have fled here because of the storm and who press themselves against the walls with each flash. In one of the flashes, I see a woman about my age in a thin, dirty dress who must have been here the whole time. I try to talk to her, but she refuses to answer. I watch the lightning flash through the slats of her house and wonder and worry about disparity and what someone like me could possibly offer someone like her. What someone like her would expect from someone like me. I dig into my pocket and find a handful of pesos, put them quietly on the ground and slip out between flashes, the storm smeared across the sky in eerie orange light.

I realize that I'm waiting for something that will never happen.

On the way back, I pass some people trying to sell avocados on the side of the road. I offer two of the mangoes I just picked for an avocado. They laugh and say it's a fair trade but they don't want mangoes and give me two avocados anyway. For nothing. Further along, I pass a *guarapo* stand – sugar cane shoved into an intricate yet clumsy assembly of cogs and belts that lurches and clatters and then dribbles thick, green juice out of one of its ends. It tastes like liquid sugar, like chewing on a branch that is still alive.

At the airport a few days later, Bill and I agree that you never know a person until you travel with them and that we are indeed ill matched. We shake hands. No kisses on cheeks or misinterpreted whispers. I watch the plane from Toronto land, the people get off, the luggage burp through tongues of slippery black plastic. The airport fills with tourists. They pick up their luggage and they go, leaving the airport suddenly empty. There is one piece of luggage

left. It is mine. I go and pick it up and bring it to the
check-in counter, ask for a window seat so that I can see
things drop away from me, hang on to them for a second,
then let them fall.

Rainy Summit

MY GRANDMOTHER DIED YESTERDAY. She was eighty-nine.

She'd been dying in increments for quite some time. First, about four years ago, she fell and broke her hip. She had it replaced and, too anxious to get things back to normal, she fell again and broke the other one. She was still living at home then, by herself. Determined. And not at all apologetic about it.

She was in a lot of pain even back then, a kind of pain that made no sense to anyone but her, not even to the handful of doctors she reluctantly saw and who ultimately gave her the diagnosis she'd known all along. Cancer. Of the bone. The 'worst' kind. Not even worth treating past the age of fifty-five because the treatment'll kill you before the cancer does. (Not that her death was at all pleasant.) So they slapped a morphine patch on her arm, told her to check into the local seniors' home, where her husband, my grandfather, was already a resident, and live her last three months under professional care.

My grandmother was quite a lady. Now, I know everyone says this, especially the day after their grandmother has died, but honest to God, she was. But I don't know how to tell you that.

~

I live in a place where it's windy most of the time. Not breezy, but somewhere between breezy and gale-force. The kind of wind where if you're outside speaking to someone, you have to raise your voice to make sure you're heard. I live on a ridge above a dead-end highway in the foothills of the Rockies, just inside a provincial park. The park extends beyond where the road ends – that's why it dead-ends. It's twenty-two kilometres from where I am to where the road ends in the summer and eleven in the winter. In the winter, they gate the road so the animals that live in the area can find more food, can migrate beyond the gate without being hit by weekend traffic from the city. It works pretty well. I've never seen any roadkill on this road, though one night last fall, a guy living close by hit two cows with his truck. Didn't even see them. He was driving past the last ranch before the park boundary, he said, and the lines on the road just disappeared where he guessed the cows had been standing. The next thing he knew, he was upside down in the ditch. Not a scratch on him. But the two cows had to be shot.

In any case, the highway is important enough that they keep it clear all year round. I like to bike – it's the thing that keeps me sane – and when I first moved here, I was pleasantly surprised to discover that I'd be able to bike through the winter, though I never expected it to last this long. It's mid-April and there's still snow on the ground. But not on the highway.

This place makes me think of my grandmother a lot. It reminds me of where she and my grandfather used to live, in Eastern Ontario, in an old converted barn, when they first retired from selling antiques. It has the same feel. The kind of place you'd live in if you wanted to be a hermit but were too scared of totally committing yourself to being one. A community nearby, but plenty of empty land in between. More chance of seeing a bear than a human on your property. A splendid view. Lots of birds to feed and listen to.

I work at a camp. In the winter, any kind of group can come up and use it, but in the summer, it's just for kids with disabilities and disease. Like diabetes. Cerebral palsy. Cancer. I'm kind of a supervisor, though that title implies more than I actually do. What I do is make sure that any group that's up here is aware that I'm around if they need help. I do this at night, and what that means is that I usually just sit in my cabin, reading, with a walkie-talkie on full volume in case anyone needs to reach me.

It was about 6:30 in the evening yesterday when I found out that my grandmother had died. My aunt called and told me the news. The sun was still high above the top of Moose Mountain, and as I walked back to my cabin, I went past a spot that overlooks the highway, and the feeling I get when I'm on my bike came to me. I felt myself riding and so I went to my cabin and got dressed to ride, got on my bike and was halfway down the path to the highway before I realized I was working. Right then. Had been for a couple of hours already. And was supposed to be on call until 10 p.m. I stopped the bike. And turned around. Took the bike back to the cabin and spent the rest of the evening perched on a railing at that spot that overlooks the highway and a picturesque valley (a splendid view, my grandmother would say), hands in my pockets, my walkie-talkie turned up loud.

I sat there and I thought about my grandmother. About what it must be like to die in pieces. First the hips, then the diagnosis, then the selling of the house and the distribution of all her treasures, which she oversaw in her fourth month in the seniors' home with remarkable clarity and equanimity. I thought about what it must be like to spend the last year and a half of your life in bed. Wanting to die but not being able to, wanting to choose when you'll die, and how, and with dignity, but not being able to. I sat there, overlooking the highway, and thought about what I could say about her that wasn't what anyone else would say about someone who'd carved herself into their life before they were even born. I couldn't think of a single thing that wasn't a cliché. Not for any other reason than that she was so big. Maybe that's why we have clichés. To describe things that are indescribable.

The radio didn't make a single noise all night. Not even a staticky squelch.

⁓

Like I said, I live in a place where wind is part of the scenery. More often than not, the noise of it wakes me up in the middle of the night. In the mornings, when I get up, the first thing I do is look at the tops of the lodgepole pines that surround the cabin to see how bent over they are. A strong wind like you get out here can make riding a bike problematic. But this morning, I set out for my ride, and the air is completely still. I can hear myself breathing, hear the headset in my bike creak when I stand on the pedals and wag the bike back and forth under me, pumping up the first hill. It's almost as if ... I don't know what. It's almost as if the wind is listening. But that sounds cliched, doesn't it?

I've had this experience with wind and death before, except in an opposite way. When my other grandmother, my father's mother, died in Germany thirteen years ago, my mother and I went over to join my dad, who'd been with her for the last couple of weeks of her life. We were at her post-burial reception, in a restaurant at the cemetery (the burial had been melodramatic, with my great-aunt Louise clinging to the coffin of her sister, shouting her name – *Maria, Maria!* – and looking at us in a beseeching manner, wondering why we all weren't doing the same) and, for some reason, after we'd finished picking at plates of food that had been placed in front of us, someone, a distant older cousin whom I'd never met, suggested that we all go shopping. Right then and there. And much to my amazement, a group of women gathered, including my mother, and we all walked from the graveyard to the nearest thoroughfare, which had a respectable (fashionable, even) department store on it. I went along because I was twenty and had never been to a funeral before, had been shocked by the cultish rituals of a religion that I'd seen my grandmother practice in public but which she had clearly never understood, and I didn't know what else to do. It felt strange, but the whole day had been strange, so in a way, going shopping felt normal. In any case, as we were walking down that main thoroughfare, about to enter the department store, a strange and sudden wind picked up. We were on the sidewalk watching an impromptu tornado whip down the street, rocking cars and sweeping up umbrellas and discarded plastic bags. It disintegrated as quickly as it had appeared, but we all stood and looked at each other as if we were all thinking the same thing: that it was Maria's spirit expressing disapproval at our behaviour (something she had done with great regularity, and which, in all honesty, felt very similar to that compact tornado). No one said anything. But clearly it was time to decide on what side of some sort of arbitrarily constructed fence each of us stood. The others went into the department store. My mother and I walked back to my grandmother's (now my father's) apartment.

That's the first thing I think of when I notice the stillness on my ride this morning. Wind. And death. How the two intertwine. It's a nice ride ... as good as it gets in these parts when the temperature is still in the single digits in the last half of April. There's no traffic, just a small group of hikers spread out in pairs over about three kilometres of the highway, walking along its shoulder, facing oncoming traffic that doesn't exist. I wonder why they're here – seems a strange place to hike – but then I remember that you don't always need a reason for doing things. That sometimes just doing them is enough.

No one in my family has ever been very good at doing something just for the sake of doing it. I've always felt I need good, solid reasons for doing anything – taking out the garbage, deciding to get a cat, going out with a certain type of man – and more often than not, I choose the activities I engage in based on a sort of righteousness. On a sort of reasoning that what I'm doing has a higher purpose. Put me in the middle of a paintball game and I just don't get it. Ask me, when I'm making a lemon tart (always for someone else, never for myself), what I'm doing, and I'll give you an answer along the lines of 'helping whoever tastes this be aware of the connection between tasting something vibrant and living life well.' Not just because I want to. It sounds pretentious, but I can't help it.

For Germans, all action that lacks a moral lesson is suspect. And while I can't say for sure, it would be pretty easy to make an assumption about where that comes from. Lessons we learn. Being of Germanic descent, I am like this in every aspect of my life, except biking. I like biking.

That's all there is to it. I don't do it because it keeps me in shape, or because it's a way of getting from A to B. I do it simply because I like it, and always have. It just so happens that while I'm doing it, I can get from A to B and stay in shape, but if biking did neither of those things, I'd still like it as much as I do. I like it so much that I take my bike wherever I go. I've been to a few different corners of the world, biking. Just because. The next place I want to go with my bike is a little island in the Indian Ocean, and the other day, when a friend asked me why I wanted to go there, I just shrugged and said, Why not? Because I'm interested. I don't know why. Couldn't tell him any more than that. That confused him. Because if *there*, why not anywhere else?

In any case, this is something I've been doing for fifteen years now. It's no secret. Here's the strange part, though. A couple of years ago, my grandmother and grandfather and I were just sitting around, talking about travelling and cycling. It was a nice summer day, just before my grandmother broke her hip the first time. The cicadas were buzzing outside, but their place was cool and dark. My grandmother had made us some ginger iced tea. Anyway, my grandfather said to me, 'You know, your grandmother did the same thing in the thirties.' I said, 'What?' My grandmother scowled at my grandfather. He said, 'She rode around Europe on her bicycle for two years, before we were married, putting together the family tree.' She waved him silent, then looked at me dead on. I stared at her with my mouth open, incredulous, and said, 'Is that true?' She said, 'Well, we didn't have a car.'

In our family, the family tree is a big deal. It's not just a sheet of paper. My grandmother managed to trace some lines back to the fifteenth century. This part I knew before a couple of years ago. This part I grew up knowing. She gathered most of the information just before the Second World War; it started as a need to prove (non-Semitic) ancestry to the German government, I think, and grew and grew, mostly because my grandmother suspected that most of the records would be destroyed if there was a war. And she was right. They were living in northern Germany then, and after she got home, my grandfather went to war and she had four daughters. On each of those daughter's fortieth birthdays, she gave them a copy of the family tree and all of the documents supporting her research – birth certificates, marriage records, etc. So that tree gets pulled out every now and then and mulled over, which is why I know about that part, but not about how she put it together.

I was flipping through all the documents a couple of months ago because I was interested in ancestry – not so much in my own direct links to it, but in a vague emotional survey of how we connect ourselves to blood. In any case, I had the documents in a big pile in front of me, and I was turning them over one by one, trying to keep them in order, when a small, orange piece of paper fell out, flipped past, floated to the ground. It was that thick, homemade kind of paper, something between construction paper and card-board, about the size of two index cards – a carbon copy of something. A telegram. It had my grandfather's name on top, and his regiment number. No location. The message read '*Wiebke geboren alles gesund sorge unnötig.*' Which means 'Wiebke born everyone healthy don't worry.'

Wiebke is my mother. My grandmother's first child. She had no idea where my grandfather was when my mother was born or, probably, if he was even alive. It was the same when all of her other daughters were born.

~

A morphine patch is like a nicotine patch, a sort of timed-release thing where if your body needs it, it gets some. Morphine manages intense pain. One patch, I've been told, generally lasts about a month. A month into her stay at the seniors' home, my grandmother was going through two every three days. The doctors told my mother and her sisters that once you go on morphine, that's pretty much the end of the story. You get delusional. They said she'd no longer be the person we knew her as. Three months, tops, they said. She starved herself that first month in the home, to no avail. She lived for another year and a half. Lucid as can be. There were moments, of course, when she was confused, maybe even delusional, but generally she was clear as a bell. Right to the end. I called her last week and she recognized my voice right away. She sounded pretty bad, and usually when she does, she asks me to call her back. She didn't this time, though, said she just wanted to be quiet on the phone with me for a while. 'Okay,' I said. And so we were quiet. After ten or fifteen minutes, I asked her if she was awake, and she said yes. 'You have to go for dinner soon,' I said. 'Yes,' she said. 'Thank you for calling.' And then we hung up. That was the last time I talked to her, and I knew it when I hung up. I cried more then than I have since I found out that she died.

So this morning, this ride I'm on is for her. For everything she did, and because she would have been on this ride at my age. For raising four daughters alone, during the war, with no food and no money. For learning how to fly a glider. For looking smashing in the sports car my grandfather bought when he was seventy. For being too big for me to describe to anyone else but in clichés.

The ride to the gate at the end of the road is slightly uphill, usually with a headwind, but like I said, there's no wind this morning. The road crosses the river just beyond the camp, passes through some meadows that moose like to hang out in (she would have liked that), then begins an undulating up and down over the bottom flank of a mountain, all the way past Canyon Creek, where, if you look at the right moment, you can see the flare from an oil pump station (she wouldn't have liked that) poking above the lodgepole pines. It's always lit. If you walk west along the ridge beyond the camp, you can see it at night, orange fingers licking black air.

Anyway, I'm riding along and it's all quiet and lonesome and then suddenly there's this squawking. I look up into the trees on the other side of the road and there's a big old raven in its nest making a whole lot of fuss. More squawking. Up ahead on my side of the road there's another raven – he's got something in his beak and the raven in the nest is none too pleased about it. Swoops down and, with wings spread, starts launching and pecking at the other one. Who ignores him. I'm thinking all the usual things: how this has to be a symbol of something, how my grandmother is in there somewhere, but I'm too sad right now to see it for sure.

By the time I ride past the ravens, the complacent one's had enough, and it launches itself back at the other one. A flurry of black and wings and feathers. I stop to watch them. They stop fighting, and stand side by side, adjusting their feathers, looking at me. Posing, almost. Damned if I know what that means. I push myself back onto the seat of my bike, then stand and pump to get going again. Behind me, I can hear the squawking starting up again. Who was it, Jim Harrison maybe, who asked how it was possible that ravens have all of their vocabulary in two notes? I like that. My grandmother would have liked that too, though I don't think she would have liked ravens. She didn't like big, bossy things, no matter how spiritually prophetic they were supposed to be. She liked little things whose impact was less brazen but just as potent. Like chickadees. Or purple martins.

Just past the meadows, just before you get to Canyon Creek, the road swings wide and stretches out straight, and along the flats there are more dots, hikers walking along. They're all spread out because they're walking at different paces. They all just smile when I say hello, passing them in high gear, the bike wagging under me. One more hill and I'll be at the gate. It's been warm lately (above freezing, anyway) and I wonder if enough snow has melted that I'll be able to ride past it.

I pump up the hill. At this point on the ride, no matter how windy it is, it's always peaceful. Or rather, you can hear the wind in the valley below, you just can't feel it. Today, all I hear is my chain slipping over the cogs and the sound of air passing in and out of my mouth. I get to the top, sit back in my seat, catch my breath, coast along the trees for a bit, then start downhill toward the gate. I pass one more hiker, who raises his walking stick in a wave when I say hello.

The road beyond looks clear. I get to the bottom of the hill, ride up to the gate and lift my bike over it. From here, the road starts uphill again, crests a pass called Rainy Summit, descends to the river again and ends. The last time I rode it was at the end of November. Five months ago. I hop on my bike and start pedalling, but I don't get very far. A couple hundred metres down the road, around a big bend, there's still snowpack. Enough that I can't ride through it. I ride up to its edge and make a slow, sweeping turn back toward where I came from.

When I get back to the gate, I see that lone hiker I passed a few minutes ago leaning against it. I hoist my bike over the gate again and he comes over to hold it while I hop over. 'What's it like up there?' he asks. 'I don't know,' I say. 'Couldn't get much past the bend.' He nods. He's a stout, squat man of about sixty-five. He's wearing one of those square olive-green caps like the ones Castro used to wear before he got all crazy about foreign investment, and it's got a huge engraved name tag on the front. *Wally*, it says, *Highway Restoration Program*. He's got on a blue work shirt, has four or five pens neatly arranged in his breast pocket, and he's wearing suspenders and, honest to God, dungarees. Not jeans. Dungarees. He's holding a stick to stab garbage with, not a walking stick.

'I've never been up there,' he says, nodding beyond the gate. 'Gosh, you live here your whole life and you think you see something new every day but you still don't get to see it all before you die, do you?' he says. He turns away. And all of a sudden, my stomach is tight and my cheeks are wet and I'm gasping. I've got my arms on the gate and my head on my arms and I'm standing there, crying.

Wally comes back to me, puts his hand on my shoulder and rubs it. 'Whatever it is, it'll be okay. Just think. You'll be able to see something new soon, maybe even up that road, and everything will seem okay,' he says. 'Everything will seem new again.' I nod, with my head still down, sniffing, breathing through my mouth, tears welling up in waves.

He pats my shoulder and walks away. When I turn around a few minutes later, he's gone.

So I get back on my bike and I start riding back home, back to the camp, still gulping, tears still coming. I look at the trees and the clear river below, flowing over rocks, between boulders, and I listen to the silence and I think about how much she would have liked this place. No reason. Just because. I know she would have.

I crest the first hill. From the top of it, the road dips to Canyon Creek and you can look up the incline of the next hill. It's the kind of view that would make a really nice picture in one of those *A-Day-in-the-Life* books, but today when I come over the top and look down that dip and up the next one, the hikers scattered all over it, small and moving toward me, toward death, and the symbolism of that gate they'll have to turn back at is too much.

I stand at the top of the hill with my mouth open, stunned, cheeks wet. I look up at the sky for something, I don't know what. I look at the road ahead and hikers are still trickling down it. A car comes over the hill facing me, about 200 yards away, cuts the corner a bit too close, almost nails one of the hikers. Honks its horn, drowning out the hiker's shout. All of the hikers turn in succession, like dominoes, to watch the car pass. It doesn't even slow down, disappears into the dip of Canyon Creek, then reappears a few seconds later, swishing past me, kicking up dirt from the opposite shoulder. I turn and watch the car until I can't see it anymore.

I have a picture of my grandmother on the wall above my desk. It's of her eightieth birthday party, and in it she's holding eighty brightly coloured balloons. Now, she was never a big woman and certainly never one to smile for photos, but in this one, she's a dwarf under all those balloons and she's got a grin on her face the size of Texas. When I got the phone call yesterday saying she'd died, that it was a good thing because she'd been in a lot of pain, I took the picture down, determined to take it with me everywhere I went until I had come to grips with her death. I have it with me now, as a matter of fact, on the ride, and when I pull it out and look at it, I know I've made a mistake. Because it's going to take a long time to do that, and looking at that wall and seeing that gap is going to be more painful than looking up and seeing her there.

I get on my bike, swing down the hill, close my eyes as I pass all the hikers. A bit of a tailwind has picked up now, and the riding's fast, silent, peaceful. I rumble over the last Texas gate before the camp and see something that looks like a destroyed beehive in the grass on the side of the road. I slow down when I see the eyes. I stop in front of it, about five feet away. It's a huge grey owl. Just sitting. And staring at me. One of its wings looks all strange, like the owl's sitting on it, but I don't know much about owls, so I can't say if it's broken or not. The owl's calm, doesn't seem concerned that I'm close. He just looks at me and blinks once, slowly. Like I have no right to have done all the stupid things I've ever done in my life.

The ranger station is near the camp, so I stop there to tell them about the owl. The ranger looks at me, smiles, and says, 'Oh, yeah ... the one that makes you feel like you haven't done anything useful in your whole life?' I nod. He says, 'All right then, I'll go take a look.' And he pulls up his collar and smooths down his shirt and straightens his cuffs, as if he's on his way to defend his character.

I'm in my cabin now, and the picture has been faithfully reinstated to its old spot, its exact spot within a yellowing frame of age on the wall. Normally when I go on a trip, I'm packed a week beforehand. In some situations when packing would not seem appropriate or tactful – say, like leaving a boyfriend – I mentally pack my suitcase every day until I leave. Picture packing it and picture seeing it packed. But this time, I'm not doing that. I'm avoiding it. It's the day I'm leaving to go back east and I haven't given it one thought. I still have to figure out a way to get into town, which could take a couple of hours, and I haven't even pulled my suitcase out. My flight leaves this afternoon, and what am I doing? I'm writing this.

Right now, it seems that even time doesn't know what to do. It stands awkwardly at the sidelines while we absorb her death. Tenses get mixed up: *She was a great person, she doesn't want a big funeral, the next time I see her ...* It forgets, like we do. But then it seems to slowly, almost imperceptibly, groan into function again, like a series of huge stone wheels at an old mill, making us aware only when we're ready (or more comfortable with the idea) that she's no longer here. That we'll no longer feel her tiny, bony, piercing hugs again, or smell the mix of ginger and saffron and chocolate and wood smoke that was the smell of her house, or watch her waving elegantly from her porch. Or taste the yeasty apple crumble thing she used to make.

We've had a couple of years to get used to those more tangible losses. But this final loss is something else.

So I get my suitcase out and start to pack with a Johnny Thunders song running through my head, and I know that he's right. You can't put your arm around a memory. A friend of mine wrote to me the other day that lineage is incorporated in a series of dreams like Russian dolls; we keep our ancestors in our dreams, and they keep theirs in their dreams. I like that. I find it comforting and wonder if my grandmother will know when I'm dreaming about her. Or if she'll orchestrate a dream with herself in it as a way of saying hello. Maybe that's what ancestors do to keep themselves alive. I hope so.

There's a saying that goes when someone dies, all that's left of them is wrong opinions or impressions of them. I don't know about that. I'm not sure how you can know everything that one person is, but I know that one day, a year from now, maybe longer, even, I'll be somewhere and everything that my grandmother meant to me that I can't describe now, that I can't have anymore, or that she couldn't even fathom she was, will come flooding over me, and that in the meantime, allowing all my memories of her to float around and crash into each other instead of nailing them down will somehow distill her personality, allow me to see who she was and is still.

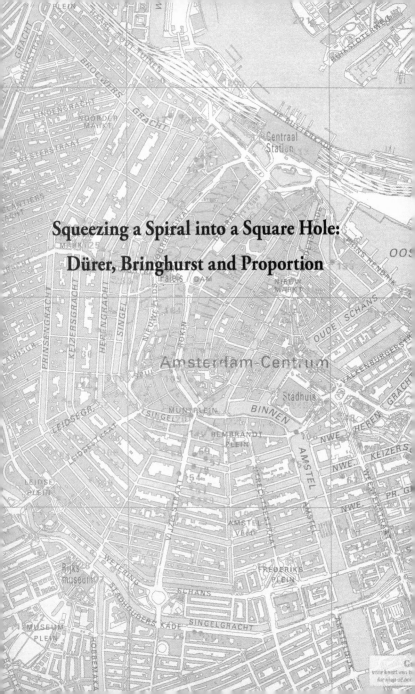

# Squeezing a Spiral into a Square Hole:

# Dürer, Bringhurst and Proportion

WE ARE IN A BAR, in Amsterdam, a *bruin* café, the local tavern. We've brought a book about Albrecht Dürer to discuss, and on the table we choose, someone has left a small stem with twinned leaves on top of some used coasters. It looks like an organic compass. The kind you'd use to draw a perfect circle. Walter, an installation artist, looks at me, and I look at him. We sit down and I flip through the book on Dürer, which has lovely, precise sepia diagrams on perspective and how to accomplish certain geometrical shapes in drawing.

For a living, I design and print books the old-fashioned way: by hand. Over dinner at Walter's apartment, I'd wondered aloud what the conscious relationship is between planning and chaos, detail and spontaneity – how one exists in the other. Can each be summoned when necessary in the creative process or is the point that it be haphazard? I have always felt an element of chaos in detail and planning in spontaneity, but that feeling itself is instinctual and not at all based in reason, so I have never quite been able to explain it. That was when Walter went straight to his bookshelf, picked out the Dürer book and said, 'Let's have a drink.'

I understand the seduction of a simple solution, of finding virtue in the most abominable flaw. I once confessed to a professional musician that I had somehow made it to the Grade 8 conservatory level in piano without being able to read a note of music, and that I had quit because that seemed fraudulent. She smiled. 'What you should have done,' she said, 'was take up jazz instead.' She was being kind, of course, but forgiveness is seductive, and it is most seductive and timeless when the proper channels have been navigated, channels that are just as easily employed in jazz as in typography or graphic design – that is to say, you have to know the rules in order to break them well or, at least, most effectively. Forgiveness is what allows us to break the rules.

I encounter wistful moments of the if-only-I-had-known-that-then kind when I refer to Robert Bringhurst's *The Elements of Typographic Style* for my work. It is masterful in its instruction. It gently nudges instead of demands, is suggestive as opposed to pedantic (though it has a pedantic purpose). Typographers fall in love with books, as Bringhurst writes, when 'structural harmony is not so much enforced as implied.' He has an uncanny ability to make a suggestion, then to hook you with a sentence like that, and suddenly you find yourself with your hands tied: you know you're going to do what he says, or at least spend more time considering his suggestion than you'd thought you would. But then, Bringhurst has one thing in his favour: those who pick up this book are mainly the already-obsessed.

I was on a bus back in Canada a couple of weeks ago and as I was paying my fare the driver winked at me in a certain way, almost as if in code. I looked at him curiously and he pointed to Bringhurst's book, which was in my other hand. I asked him if he was a printer and he said no, he just loved type and fonts, and over the next two hours of our trundle up the Sunshine Coast, he disclosed his preferences in typefaces – serif over sans serif, long ascenders and descenders over the Venetian 'e' – and called Bringhurst's book 'the definitive book on type and design, period.' You hear this a lot in printing and graphic design circles, but not so much on a bus doing a milk run in coastal B.C. It was a moment to savour, and if Bringhurst's desire for democratic appeal is as honest as he says it is, I think he would have been proud to hear the tribute coming from that man.

*The Elements of Typographic Style* begins with a visual historical synopsis of how our letters have changed – from the pen-formed terminals of the Renaissance through the Baroque, Neoclassical and Romantic influences to sans-serif realism and rationalist postmodernism. The principles he lays out are concise, well-founded, easy to follow. '1.1.1. Typography exists to honor content' gives way to '1.1.3. There is a style beyond style.' The deeper into the book you go, the more detailed he gets: '5.1.4. Consider even the lowly hyphen.' Bringhurst begins with a rigid structure, then shows you how to move around in it.

You discover in the text a lot of what you already know but sometimes don't want to: that 'Why not?' is rarely enough of a reason to break a rule. Or rather, that it's a tempting justification when you're young and inexperienced, but rarely effective enough that it stands the test of time. And nowhere is that more clear than in Dürer, contemporary abstract art and Bringhurst's discussion of the golden section.

Back at the bar, Walter tells me about the modular ruler he made while he was studying at an art academy – a ruler with a prearranged set of harmonious proportions as opposed to equal units of measurement – and the compass he made whose purpose was solely to create an ellipse. Not a circle, but an ellipse. There's a shine to his eye now, and he starts grabbing coasters, sketching madly on them to illustrate what an elliptical compass is and how it works. I'm thinking that even if I hadn't once taken refuge in the idea of right answers, even if I didn't have this love for equations that I can't explain, even if I was not able to follow his logic, I would love this man for all the passion that's coming from the fingers of his left hand, from what is spilling from his pen onto those coasters.

The idea of the elliptical compass came from Leonardo da Vinci, of course, and it's not as easy to use as it sounds. It has three legs, Walter says – he picks up the twinned leaf and adds his pen to its apex to make a triton – two with points to pivot on and the other to draw with. You have to draw it in steps, switching the points without actually moving the position of the drawing tip, to create the perfect ellipse.

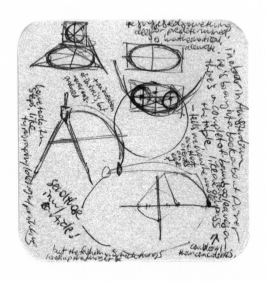

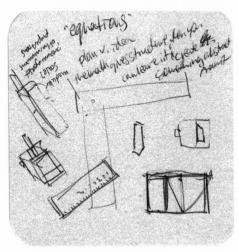

We talk about *the math* versus *the idea* and he tells me that he thinks you need the math to give you your image, your idea its structure, but that at some point you have to abandon accuracy in numbers and create something abstract from your knowledge. That abstract thing can still be incredibly accurate, he says, but you have to inherently understand the math in order to throw it away and let your instinct take over. The math will still be there, but only subconsciously, and it will make the abstract thing good. The rule is that the math needs to stay in the background. He tells me about another book he has at home, a thick Piet Mondrian catalogue he'd received as a gift once. Mondrian, he says, used the structure of his studio as a test for his work, painting a white square with black stripes around it on a grey wall, et cetera. There was a wood stove in his studio for heat and he hated that thing because it was round – it was the only thing in there that wasn't square or straight-edged. 'Of course, for artists, Mondrian is a very important person to study,' Walter says, 'but I think you should just look at it and forget it.'

~

Go to your bookshelf and pull out your favourite book. Not your favourite story or your favourite author, but your favourite book to hold, to sit in a chair with and read, to flip slowly through with the phone unplugged. Open it up – any page will do. What is it that makes it a pleasure to hold and to read? It's probably difficult to say, and part of you senses that knowing might ruin the experience.

Most design is convenience-based: making the most of standardized press-sheet sizes, and is therefore bland. But every now and then, we're all drawn to a certain book or page layout, and most of us don't know why. There is a difference between not noticing something because it is standard, unremarkable ('There are [also] those who think that putting chairs and air-conditioners in hell will make it just as good as heaven,' Bringhurst says), and not noticing something because it has been well designed. There's a reason certain books look and feel good to the eye. It almost always has to do with proportion in design. In books, as with most visual things, what makes a page attractive and easy to read, its design invisible, is proportion. And the *pièce de résistance* of proportion is the golden section.

The golden section is an ancient proportion found in nature. It is a symmetrical relation made from asymmetrical parts, and occurs when the ratio of the smaller part to the larger part is the same as the larger part is to the sum [i.e. a:b = b:(a+b)]. The ratio (1:1.61803) gives us the value of $\Phi$ (phi), an irrational number with qualities of spiralling logarithms and the quantification of unchecked propagation. The easiest way to picture the golden section in nature is to imagine the cross-section of a nautilus shell, growing outward neatly, beautifully, in perfect proportion to the previous layer of spiral. It is this relationship that is ever appealing to us, whether in the form of the human body or in musical scales, or in the relationship of text to a page. Bringhurst's discussion of the golden section is crucial to the understanding of design, and of why certain things work and others don't. In other words, if double-square books (i.e., books whose width:length proportion is 1:2) look good to you, it's probably because the relationship of proportion is the same relationship as that found between the notes in a simple octave: a 'primary visual chord' has been created, according to Bringhurst. Clearly, not everything needs to relate back to the exact proportions of the golden section (imagine how bland uniform beauty would be), but what Bringhurst does is nudge us toward an explanation of why certain proportions might be attractive to us, because, he proposes, they are innate and appear so subtly in things around us that we don't even notice them. In a well-designed book or page, he says, 'the text takes precedence over the purity of the design, and the typographic texture of the text takes precedence over the absolute proportions of the individual page.' And, he adds, if you choose to have non-traditional proportions, you should do so with 'a clear and purposeful degree.'

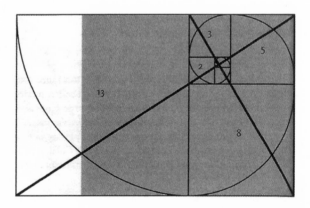

A good design will mix math and spontaneity, exactness and free-hand proportions, because the eye needs to be directed, but it also needs to have room to wander so it doesn't feel manipulated or stuck. The golden section and proportional relationship is merely a place to begin to understand why. '[A]n organic page looks and feels different from a mechanical page,' says Bringhurst, 'and the shape of the page itself will provoke certain responses and expectations in the reader, independent of whatever text it contains.' In choosing the proportions of type and spacing as well as the proportions of the page, a harmony should be suggestive, not obvious. The relationship of proportion that the designer creates among those elements will more often than not determine whether the reader feels connected to, or turned off by, a book.

~

Dürer, it turns out, also used his explorations of proportion and perspective to design typefaces. (The spiral of possibility, it seems, is both imploding and exploding.) Walter talks and I understand and we look around the bar, taking in the tableau of the twin-leafed compass and the detritus of empty, wine-stained glasses and a stack of scribbled coasters that lies before us now, as well as the Dürer book, open to a diagram on how to calculate and account for peripheral vision in the viewer when creating a drawing, and yes, you could call all this coincidence, or even just sequence, but the fashion in which these things line themselves up tonight suggest something deeper, predetermined

– yes, mathematical, accurate. Most of all, unavoidable. A sort of unchecked propagation.

A few weeks later, we meet at the same *bruin* café. I ask him what he wants to drink and go to the bar to order. When I come back to the table, there, sitting where the stem with twinned leaves had been, is a small, beautiful handmade box. Handmade by him, I know, for me. He tells me to open it. Inside is a new invention. A proportional compass. It has three legs like the elliptical compass, but one of the legs is shorter, attached two-thirds of the way down the inside of another leg.

If I'm measuring the length of something – he shows me by placing all of the points against the edge of the table, where it's easier to see the relationship between them – the middle leg will fall at exactly the place of the Golden Ratio. It will tell me what the proportional width should be: what the dimensions of the book I'm making should be or where the text block I'm placing on the page should sit. If I'm a good, experienced designer, it will tell me what I had already suspected, and will help to rein things in a bit. With this, everything will look beautiful, and this will tell me those things without any measurement, calculator, ratios, fractions or cross-multiplication or division. That is the most marvellous part. It, like Bringhurst's instruction, is something whose calculations start tight as the core or inner chamber of a nautilus shell, then open the possibility – for both the designer and the appreciator – up into an endless, ever-expanding spiral of experience. But the freedom of that experience, Bringhurst says, 'is denied us if the tradition is concealed or left for dead. Originality is everywhere, but much originality is blocked if the way back to earlier discoveries is cut or overgrown.' I don't *have* to use it in the end, but it is a classic place from which to begin. And the ironic thing is that even though part of the tradition, the mathematics of it, is marvellous – the equations and madness and obsession with the discovery of proportion – eventually, Walter says, the math gets boring, and the compass is what will let me forget the rules while respecting them. The precision has to slip away so that what matters most is the text or image on the page. It is exactly like jazz. It bops and squeals and roils and you play or listen and beam but you never, ever ask how it's done. That knowledge – that part of the process – is long past and you are entirely satisfied just being there to put your fingers on it, to listen, or look, or read: to appreciate it.

# Like Landscape Didn't Matter

'It is a terrible thing to be free. Nations know this; churches know this. People, however, seek to skirt the knowledge. They elevate freedom to a Holy Grail, disregarding the truth that constraints are what define us, in life and in language alike: we yearn to be sentenced.'

– Claire Messud, *The Last Life*

THERE'S A STRONG WIND BLOWING in Amsterdam this morning, strong enough that the streets are empty of even the most committed cyclists, which is saying a lot. There hasn't been a frost yet this winter, and it might be easy to extrapolate that this wind is part of the global warming trend, but the fact is Dutch winters are unruly at best, so it's hard to say.

I'm biking over a bridge that parallels the ring road, the A2 highway, which is gridlocked. I once heard ring roads described as modern versions of Dante's nine circles of Hell, each designed to torture the greedy consumers in its own way, a description that's hard not to smile at. Even though it's difficult to say what's the result of global warming and what isn't, it always amazes me that a wind like this isn't enough to get us to think twice about how we live our lives – but then, if history is an indicator, money and self-interest always win. I look at that jammed highway and a scene in *The Magnificent Ambersons* comes to mind, the one where Joseph Cotton says, 'Automobiles have come, and almost all outward things are going to be different because of what they bring. They're going to alter war, and they're going to alter peace. And I think men's minds are going to be changed in subtle ways because of automobiles,' and how nuts everyone he was sitting with thought he was.

I'm heading to my least favourite part of Amsterdam, a place called IJburg. It's a new suburb built on water – landfill that creeps into a large inland lake called the IJsselmeer. The IJsselmeer itself was once part of the North Sea before the Dutch blocked it off with a thirty-kilometre-long dike after an enormous flood in 1916. It's a strange place, this IJburg, and while I hate it, I also find it fascinating. But then, I've been reading a lot of Jim Harrison lately to allay the kind of homesickness that tends to set in after a year or so in a densely populated place – a homesickness not for a specific place, but merely for a wide open space (which, ironically, is what IJburg once was). I usually go for rides down the Amstel River where, ten minutes from Amsterdam's core, a countryside that seems unchanged since Rembrandt's time reveals itself. Going to IJburg is sure to make my homesickness worse, but things like that tend to help me find my character again, make me realize what I love and can connect to, and there's a comfort in that sort of mild masochism.

IJburg is a suburb being built on seven manmade islands to house, eventually, 45 000 people. Its completion date is 2012, and I count thirty-three cranes across the skyline of the three islands that have been built so far. It's accessible only by bridge, and somehow that seems appropriate: a neighbourhood so progressive and modern, without a shred of history, must remain separate from the completely opposite stereotype of the city that spawned it.

If you look across the water from that main bridge, you see a row of old, tilted houses that were built on a fifteenth-century dike. A stumpy clock tower struggles to be the tallest building, its polished weathervane glinting, an indication of care. Countless masts of ancient sloops rise against the shore, boats like this one that used to carry cargo to places isolated by water – before roads, trains, highways, trucks, cars, before gridlock. When you look at that town, Durgerdam, from a distance, you're not sure whether you're looking at something that exists now or a ghost of 200 years ago. If you pan to the right, though, a tall sleek white windmill – the kind used on wind farms today – spinning furiously in this morning's wind, brings you back to the present day, and the noise from the ring road fills your ears again. But at first glance, nothing could be more opposite from IJburg than Durgerdam. Across the bay, sleepy smoke rises from chimneys; the sun, you imagine, passes through infinite dust particles before hitting the old wooden floorboards of kitchens and of the local coffeehouse, where the aroma of bread rises and steam curls upward from cups held by hands made cold by the damp.

Over in IJburg, no one is around. The place is still under construction, but people started moving in nearly five years ago, their presence indicated only by bicycles locked outside entranceways or the occasional abandoned toy truck in front of a ground-floor window. Slabs of concrete stand bare, abstract, surrounded by makeshift fences made from spare rebar or scaffolding. All-glass offices stand empty, a single piece of drywall unpainted among pillars and an unfinished concrete floor, a screwdriver forgotten by the door. There are plenty of cars, parked and driving around, but no humans; apparently 5,000 people live here now. You wouldn't know it. I moved here from a Canadian town, population 800, spread out over a few kilometres. It was easier to see humans there – people who were self-described hermits. The only sign of life here, on a Monday morning at 11, is a small group of kids playing in the concrete yard of a school that sits in the middle of a construction zone. The school is perfect, finished within its fences and walls, with chaos – a mud pit, piles of landfill – surrounding it, as though the school were an oasis of perfection, or at least completion. An alarm sounds somewhere in a faraway underground parking lot, echoing, it seems, through the whole suburb. No one tending to it.

The whole place feels like a shiny new ghetto. Oddly enough, though, there is one of those ancient sloops – the kind that populate historic villages like Durgerdam – docked in front of a newly inhabited condo building, and it doesn't look strange with all IJburg's cranes rising high behind it. Maybe because it's the one thing that provides a sort of humanness that I desperately want to see.

While I'm staring at the sloop – a *tjalk*, in Dutch – two construction workers, harnessed, because of the wind, to the scaffolding five storeys above me, wave and yell at me to fix my hair. Ha ha. Soon after, a pounding starts, the kind a migraine would feel like – but this one is exterior, and felt through the feet. An enormous piledriver jams away close by, the sound so loud it forces me to blink with the force of each pounding.

The manmade beach at IJburg is called Blijburg. *Blij* in Dutch means happy, and, standing on the beach, I'm not certain whether it was named with tongue in cheek, or in

a state of hopefulness or optimism. I have to walk through a construction zone to get there, and the beach itself is small and dirty, its outer perimeter, where one would want to wander out to its natural end, blocked off by an eight-foot-high chain-link fence that extends into the water.

There's a sign in the middle of the beach, precisely at the shore's edge: No Swimming Allowed.

Despite this, two women have found a spot on a concrete breakwater at Blijburg's edge and are have a picnic amid the rubble, noise and wind. Two more *tjalk*s, moving in the distance under reefed sails, skitter across the horizon, and Durgerdam shimmers in a flash of sun breaking through fast-moving clouds.

After a while, the noise stops. The wind whistles through all the blank but semi-occupied streets in a way that can only be apocalyptic. On the main strip, an LCD board promises that the LRT from Centraal Station will be here in eleven minutes. I look around and see no indication that this could be true. The tram lines don't hum, no one is waiting patiently at its stops. Why would it come? But it will. In ten minutes now.

⌐

I used to think that I could bear any kind of loss – a limb, sight, the love of my life – but memory. That kind of loss leaves you with nothing but starting over, which seems like an insult. I'm now at an age where I'm noticing that my memory is not what it used to be. You think memory is like anything else, that it gets better with practice, and it can, but it's a bit strange. We tend to think of it as either a straight line or bubbles of past experience that touch nothing else unless something forces us to connect them. I think it's more like that stone wall that the sculptor Andy Goldsworthy built, the one that starts at a four-lane highway and runs straight, straight, directly away from it, bolting across a huge empty field. It only begins to twist and turn, like a river, when it enters a forest, which is where it starts to form itself to the landscape, to the obstacles in its path. On the inside we shape our memory wherever it'll fit. On the outside it's the shortest line between two points. Maybe when I was younger I was on the outside. Maybe I'm on the inside now. Funny thing is, I've discovered that I don't mind losing memory as much as I always thought I would. I think it's hugely important, but it can also wind up being a bit masturbatory. Maybe it's enough to remember why it's important. Like landscape.

On my way back into Amsterdam, church bells are ringing somewhere in the centre at one of the big churches. A bright orange easyJet plane flies overhead, north to London, maybe. An enormous container barge glides through the Rhine Canal, heading southeast toward Germany. Smoke continues to rise from the houses on the dike of Durgerdam, and the pounding has begun in IJburg again. The collision of all these things is too much to analyze in this brief moment – they merely exist simultaneously, side by side. But I'm reminded of something Simon Schama said in his book *Landscape and Memory*, that 'to see the ghostly outline of an old landscape beneath the superficial covering of the contemporary is to be made vividly aware of the endurance of core myths.' Durgerdam, IJburg. Fifteenth century, twenty-first. Memory and myth versus a blank slate. Something discardable versus something embraceable.

I used to be obsessed with the illogical or anachronistic in places like India, where modernity frequently skips decades of development that the Western world has endured. From candlelight to high-speed internet overnight, for instance, or mule travel to a surge in low-cost jet travel. In post-Soviet Georgia, progress was at a standstill, and decay, while far from charming, coated everything, but things were still used despite their condition because they were all anyone had. Nothing was abandoned, though everything had an abandoned feel. When I look at IJburg, I see the same tinges of abandonment, even decay, though none of the dedication to utility. A phrase of Harrison's that I read the other day pops into mind: 'People make terrible messes pretending they're perfect.' Faced with the most extreme examples, it's now easier for me to see the subtle signs of progress in the West. They're there, just as in India or Georgia, but easier to ignore.

I often have the unsettling feeling that we harness ourselves to the future, to prospects and the machinery we invent to propel and keep us there. The car, for instance, or telecommunication. There's no doubt that these things make our lives easier, but I question their now-unquestionable necessity. 'For if,' Schama says, 'the entire history of landscape in the West is indeed just a mindless race toward a machine-driven universe, uncomplicated by myth, metaphor and allegory, where measurement, not memory, is the absolute arbiter of value, where our ingenuity is our tragedy, then we are indeed trapped in the engine of our self-destruction.'

A friend asked recently if I'd ever been to Vegas, and I confessed that it is one of the few places in the world I feel I can miss, but that my dad had recently sold our family boat to invest in a house there, though he was lost without water and disliked gambling. His compulsions lie elsewhere, I said, and it's a relief to know that. My friend asked if I would go and visit him there and I said I wasn't sure. It's difficult to ignore my disdain for a place built on excess, I said. He asked if maybe I was afraid of a place where discretion was optional. I shook my head. The hope that things will change can be more damaging than the compulsions (the harmful ones) themselves, and Vegas seems to me to be derivative of that kind of hope.

But there's hope and then there's hope. IJburg's is of a different kind. The point was to build a place where community rules, where the negative aspects of human nature are ignored or very deliberately not taken into account, where bikes can be left outside overnight, unlocked, for days without worry. IJburg is full of vision, a product of the Dutch tendency toward a kind of human engin-eering beyond North American comprehension, where human behaviour is largely thought to be controllable by idealism. But at the same time it's a vision that, for me, at least, has a blank, concrete stare. It teases at progressive-ness, yet is austere. Empty. Waiting. Piles are being deaf-eningly pounded, pounded, pounded into manmade land reclaimed from the lake that was reclaimed from the sea. *Dunk dunk dunk*, so loud it prevents one from thinking. Bright construction lights on cranes keep the place under inadvertent surveillance twenty-four hours a day. At the moment (and for the last four years), IJburg is an industrial park aspiring to peaceful, fulfilling modern living, but that aspiration gets lost in the blankness.

Back in the city, on the street I'm riding along, there's a row of attached, condemned houses. It takes up the whole block and all the doors have been removed and the windows taken out so you can see its insides without obstruction or glare - revealing a sort of privacy of a person's recent past, without the person. Like going into someone's room after they've died and not being able to ask them why they thought purple would look good.

There must be fifty or sixty houses on the block, each with three storeys, each storey a different apartment. Every hold shows something different: a yellow bathroom with a large unpainted square above the floor where the cupboard and sink used to be; a living room wall painted with the handprints of children – at least three different sizes, fingers outspread, lifelines betrayed to strangers and voyeurs; a tiled kitchen with an old photo of Mao still tacked to the wall; a bedroom with a cross burned into its back wall, the one that would have overlooked the courtyard that was once there.

It's eerie and exciting at the same time – the kind of thing you want to consider only during the daytime. The kind of thing you want to rush past at night. A friend of mine who has spent his whole life in crowded European cities told me he drove across Canada once – the idea was to take it easy, do it at a leisurely pace, but the first time he drove off the road and stopped in the middle of nothing to see what the middle of nothing would be like, it (a l l   t h a t   s p a c e) terrified him so much that he ran back to the car and drove for three and a half days without rest, stopping for fuel only at gas stations with a lineup of people. I never understood his feeling until I passed this row of abandoned houses in the middle of the night. The whole block was cast in darkness, which would have been fine in the middle of nothing on the prairie, but here it felt like a place that was unsure of its next incarnation: a dangerous sort of purgatory. A place suspended between the past and the future, the indelible and the temporary, but numb to the present. I think that's what my friend felt in the vast landscape of Canada, somewhere near Wawa. A numbness. Not in himself, but in the land. He encountered, perhaps, 'a point in our identity that would require a much deeper delving and a more radical return.'

‑

The row of houses is being torn down. An excavator with an extra-long arm is going at them one by one with its shovel, crushing and crumbling the brick, the wallpaper, the parquet floors, the graffiti painted on walls while they stood abandoned.

A few of us have stopped on the road, relinquishing time for fascination, to watch the excavator work. It seems so brutish, like an elk ramming a tree to get its rack off its head. But the operator occasionally stops his grand, storey-crumbling sweeps, opens the mouth of the shovel a tiny bit, swivels it ninety degrees like a carnival-goer operating one of those machines where you try to pick up a stuffed animal in a glass case, and moves it toward a single floorboard, or a piece of wire or rebar. Then he closes the shovel around it delicately and pulls, and swivels the whole excavator around to gently place this small thing of value on a separate pile behind him. Then he goes back to ramming and smashing.

The excavator is taking down about four units a day. Every time I pass by, different wallpaper is exposed, a different bathroom is crumbling, tiles slipping soundlessly to the ground beneath the excavator's roar. The surprising vertical arc of a staircase visible, excavated now, where brick once met a plaster wall.

By now, the people who live on that street are used to it. They're tired of seeing anonymous histories exposed – they've had enough reminders of the collisions of our tendencies toward both individuality and the generic. They've stopped wondering where all of these people have dispersed to, whether they live in a similar place now,

laid out in the same way as the old one, or (a depressing thought) that even if they don't, they still probably live generically in a house with a bed, a fridge with milk in it, a stove that needs cleaning, a table and four chairs, a television. Newspapers stacked somewhere. Too many bills. Maybe even in IJburg. As though the crumbling befits the numbness, making it obvious that the only way to reconstruct involves that radical return of sorts – to a past that never quite existed for them (the residents), or us (the observers). Something that is approachable only as an impossible thing.

The wind is really strong now. I mean something you can attach a force number to. I lived in the foothills of the Rockies for a while, near Bragg Creek, where wind that makes it difficult just to stand can come off the mountains for ten days straight, but that has nothing on this. I'm struggling to get home on my bike and trees are coming down all around, hitting ground so sodden it receives them with a loud slap rather than a thump or vibration. Tarps ripped from construction scaffolding are filling the air with reverberating loud snaps the sound of inflicted pain, like rattling machine gun fire. But everyone's still driving. I suppose it's safer in a car than out on the street, until I see the largest tree on the block come down on one waiting at a traffic light.

Roof crushed to the level of the door handles. Driver somehow alive and unhurt. No one abandons their cars. The trees keep coming down. Clay tiles are being flung off roofs everywhere, smashing onto sidewalks, pavements, cars. I wonder what the wind is like in IJburg, which is much more exposed than the centre of Amsterdam. I wonder what it's doing to all that new construction, all that torn-up ground. The uncontrollable in the controlled.

~

The other day I passed an old warehouse – it had been abandoned some time ago, but suddenly there were cars and small trucks parked in a semi-circle around one of its back entrances, and people moving in and out. I stopped and asked someone what was going on. It was an anti-alternative art fair, he said, and they were setting up. I went inside: the space had been divided into convention-like booths, and pieces were being hung or constructed in their spaces. Off in the corner, there was a curtained-off area; I stepped inside and was slowly, eerily surrounded by a diaphanous cloud of coloured fog. Most of it hung near the feet, but even so, the two other people walking around the room were barely visible. Their forms were dark against the fog, as though they had no colour themselves, or what colour they'd had bled into the air, which was first flesh-coloured, then shifted to green, then brown.

The space reminded me of the surprises in Amsterdam, and I liked it. I'm talking about the surprises in its urban landscape, like the nineteenth-century village on the dike, the voyeurism of abandoned buildings. I'm not speaking metaphorically – I mean the struggle between personal expression and commercial imperatives that cities have to deal with all the time.

Amsterdam is a city that loves text. Its buildings are inscribed with it, from a short poem by Emily Dickinson on the side of a small hotel to wartime epitaphs and tenant-installed graphic design on canal houses. Poetry is by far the most prevalent, though it's done subtly enough that it often takes passing by a building a few times to notice it. I've taken to standing in front of buildings, old and new, that seem worthy of a carved verse, and then looking for it. I find it more often than not. That's the kind of surprise I'm talking about.

Or the surprises you find in changes of light. It's true what they say about Dutch light. I've never been in a place where shadow or brightness can change a landscape so much. In *Holland*. Flat and green is flat and green, you say, but on the right day... Sure the mountains in B.C. and Alberta look different in first snow, or after a warm, dry spring. But in a mesmerizing way. You expect them to look different, so you look for the differences, the subtleties. And they still hold their shape. In pancake fields you expect nothing to change. But it does – with a certain amount of shadow and sunlight, suddenly you see all the undulations in that flat land, just like you begin to see the subtleties of progress after being in its opposite extreme.

~

The storm is over now, the city scattered with trees, roof tiles, ruined cars, detritus. A friend emailed the other day about the new, alarming and frequent phenomenon of thunder-snowstorms, about how unnatural they feel. That's how this wind felt too. In Bragg Creek, in the foothills, the wind reaches hurricane force several times a year, but you almost don't feel it. Yes, it's hard to stand in it, but the wind has room to disperse, and while certainly humbling, it isn't terrifying like in a city, where hubris takes precedence over natural phenomenon. Where we have to be careful because what we have done might just kill us.

Now, Amsterdam has a reputation for über-tolerance, and there is a certain laissez-faire attitude here, but its urban identity has had a commercial imperative. For nearly half a millennium, all that mattered was making money, in a way that made Amsterdam and the Dutch famous for their frugality. But lately, personal expression has seeped in – in pot bars, in legalized prostitution, yes, yes, but other things too. I see it as a natural reaction to Dutch conservatism (for in Holland, Amsterdam is a bit of a wild child) and, I think, so do the Dutch, and that's why they allow it. They know they have a fascination with control, and under Nazi occupation they saw the limit, so personal expression acts as a sort of pressure valve, and it works, so nobody complains.

IJburg was supposed to be a neighbourhood where personal expression ruled. It didn't want to be like the rest of Amsterdam, where, no matter what the ideal, the result always wound up being the same: a place with little community and human interaction where people kept to themselves because it felt safer. Not bad, but not the original vision.

There was an article in the newspaper a couple of days ago about how IJburg had already failed. Cars were being broken into, bikes were being stolen and 'suspicious' characters (one of whom was the superintendent of IJburg, who didn't actually live or have an office there yet) were lurking about. The 5,000 residents of IJburg have had to start locking their bikes before the place is even close to completion.

They seemed annoyed to discover that human nature has prevailed again over the ideal, and they've responded with predictable human – or at least Amsterdam-like – nature: friendly on the street, but keep to yourself, lock the door and don't do anything about it. Just like in the rest of Amsterdam. Problem is, there just aren't that many people out on the street. If there had been, maybe IJburg would have stood a chance.

And maybe it still does. Maybe it'll find its own unique form of personal expression, of carving poetry into its buildings or, for the next few years, its scaffolding. Maybe it'll find its own way to respond to and embrace the decay that is already in action. Maybe the outward look, over the water, toward Durgerdam, is the answer. Maybe they'll find the answer without, in landscape, and not within, among the high-rise condo buildings. After all, as Schama says, 'it is our shaping perception that makes the difference between raw matter and landscape,' and 'memory may help to redress the balance … the cultural habits of humanity have always made room for the sacredness of nature.' I hope so, but I'm not so sure. We *are* masters of melding as a means toward progress, and landscape's where I'd look. And I'll tell you why. Because I was on the train the other day, and there was a sundog hovering in the sky, to the left. It's the kind of thing I expected to disappear as the train's angle to the sun changed, refracting the light, dissolving the optical illusion, but it stayed there, to the left, for a really long time. We must have been travelling in a perfectly straight line across those perfectly flat fields, or following the arc of the sun. We passed through a wind field, blades sweeping through the air, and I thought of that industry art fair I had seen. I thought of all the artists sitting on the black-felt platform in the warehouse, canvasses in the form of flat screens of all sizes behind them bearing images of real things, the artists with their backs turned to their work, sipping from bottles of beer set among the cables running down from the screens and stringing all over the floor like consequence; and in a corn-field the sundog disappeared and we passed through the landscape like it didn't matter.

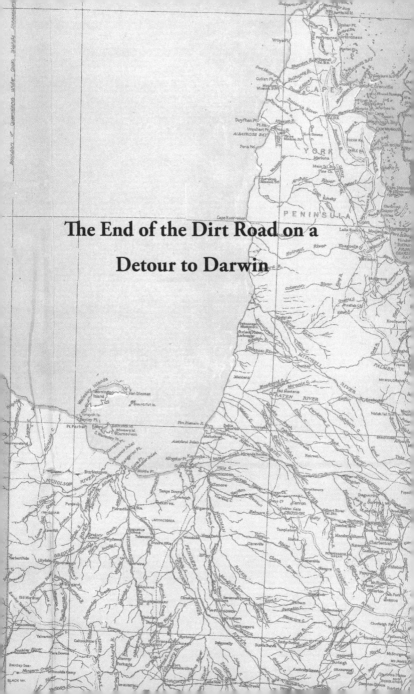

# The End of the Dirt Road on a

# Detour to Darwin

WE WERE GOING TO DRIVE TO DARWIN, and it's a long drive, but I wanted to see something authentic. I did not want to go to Alice Springs, and then drive another 400 kilometres to see a rock. I did not want to visit a sheep ranch. I wanted to see real Aussies. Not surfers or sheilas or men with cork hats. Just something completely un-stereotypical, something that might give me more of a glimpse into the Aussie psyche than a *National Geographic* article would. And so it was that I came upon a sodden, once-good-looking soul in a bar. He seemed interesting, like he had a story, and so I started a conversation with him. He was from Normanton, and I said, where's that, and he said, ah it's in the finest part of Australia. It's on the Gulf of Carpentaria, he said, and immediately my ears perked up because doesn't that just sound like a place no one would visit? It's quiet there, he said, but it sure is beautiful – the ocean is close, it's warm all year round, and the landscape! But, he said, if you really want to go someplace special, you should go just a little further down the road to Karumba. There's no more perfect an Australian word than Karumba, particularly when a half-drunk Aussie mutters it in the midst of a conversation about experiencing authenticity. The folks there will treat you right, he said, and you'll want to stay longer than you can imagine. How come I've never heard of it, I asked, and he said, it's a bitch to get to. And thus the hook was set.

The next day, we struck out for Karumba. There were three of us – old school-friends – in a classic Australian station wagon (a white Kingswood), and a crazy Swiss Guard (who was on a suspiciously vague leave of absence – we never did ask why) on a dirt bike who would pop wheelies with disconcerting regularity. And we drove and we drove. We drove for days through the plain, which was unbearable in its unending stretched-outedness. We got so bored that we took turns sitting on the roof of the Kingswood while going eighty down the dirt road, west, west toward the Gulf and the pearl of Karumba, the Swiss Guard revving beside us, encouraging us to step from the roof of the moving car to the seat of his moving dirt bike, which he drove while standing on said seat. It was easier than you'd think, and so we got good at it. We also got good at all three of us being on the roof, a brick on the accelerator, driving with a leg stuck inside the window, one toe on the steering wheel. There wasn't much traffic to worry about, see.

All of this is to say that we were young and stupid and gullible and, yes, bored. And all we really wanted was to find a place that would entertain us in a way that no other could, in a way that we had never anticipated. And after two months of travelling around Australia, we hoped that place would be Karumba, because that place hadn't been Sydney, and it hadn't been Brisbane or Cairns – the obvious ones – and we knew it wouldn't be Darwin. It had to be somewhere in between, and in Australia, *in between* often means in the middle of nowhere. Literally and figuratively.

And so we came into Karumba. We had passed through Normanton, arms waving out the windows of the Kingswood in a salute to our lonely friend in exile in a bar on the east coast, and kept driving. We were giddy. Karumba was near. We could smell change, we could taste the small fear and excitement of the unexpected.

*Unexpected* is a good word. Let me go over the adjectives our Normanton friend had used to describe Karumba and area once again: *fine, quiet, beautiful, warm, special.*

Karumba was a dump. It was the trailer park of trailer parks. There was a bar there, and, well, nothing else. The Gulf of Carpentaria lapped threateningly at the town's edge. The air was soggy, heavy with a stench of salt, death (human?) and rotten fish. A strong, furnace-like wind blew through town, and, Christ, there really was tumbleweed tumbling through the sad spaces between Karumba's houses, all of which were in various states of abandonment or boarded-upedness. We cruised slowly down the main street (okay, the only street) in about five seconds, then turned around and cruised back. We sat in the car and looked at each other. There was no need to say, *This is it?* Our Swiss Guard pulled up on his dirt bike and looked in the window. Dis is it? he said. This was it. And we were the only people around. We cruised back out to the edge of town (okay, a block away), where we'd seen a rest area, and we parked the car. We got out and leaned against it and looked around. Despite the humidity, there was dust everywhere. We were filthy from our drive, but the ocean – grey, foamy, chemical, laden with human flotsam (one metric ton of plastic bags, cigarette butts, sewage) and somehow made completely inaccessible by a series of what looked like traplines or booby traps – was not going to get us any cleaner. So we walked into the shack that served as a public washroom to see if there was running water. The shack, which had undoubtedly fallen into a state of disrepair before it was even completed, was thick with slime. The floor, the walls, the sink, the toilet: everything was green and wet. I went over to the sink to turn the tap on. A trickle of brown water, then a large groan, a spurt, and out came 264 tiny frogs. Then more brown water. Our Swiss Guard pissed in the toilet and flushed. We gathered around him and watched more frogs being spat out from around the rim. The bowl was suddenly filled with them, scrambling to get out of that cesspool of human waste. We all considered the symbolism of this, gulped, went pale and walked back outside.

It seemed obvious what we had to do. We would drink. Or at least have one drink. And if the grandeur of Karumba did not make itself apparent to us by then, we would leave. We left the car and the bike at the shack of frogs and walked to the bar. We stepped inside. The entire population (or at least a healthy representation) of Karumba was there – a dozen folk, all so drunk their heads were resting heavily on tables sticky with decades of spilled draft. Someone looked up at us with half-lidded eyes and stringy hair plastered to his cheek. Whaauuuph … , he mumbled, and thus we were officially welcomed to Karumba. His head made an astonishingly loud thump against the table.

There was no bartender. There was no music. Only the wind, the fan spinning overhead and the sound of twelve drunks well beyond their REM cycles. Our Swiss Guard hopped over the bar and looked for bottled beer. None. He poured us draft. We sat and drank gingerly out of cloudy glasses, looking out at the ocean and wondering why these people were here. Our friend had been right, we said. It sure was quiet. And *beautiful* is such a subjective term. As is *warm*. And *special*.

You wanted zumzing real, said the Swiss Guard, raising his beer and looking at me. He was right.

*You'll want to stay longer than you can imagine.* I looked around me and thought, This is a place where nothing is possible. And therefore everything is possible. It was a wide open space of *fuck everything*. And why wouldn't you want to be here? Here you could do anything you wanted, and no one would care. Here you could live your fullest dream, and it wouldn't matter to anyone but you. And if that dream involved drunkenness or amphibians or an investigation into the human condition, so much the better. This would be where you would want to be.

Karumba was beautiful because it was ugly. It was beautiful because it was real. There was no make-up, no shininess to it. It was entirely raw. There was no pretense. It was beautiful because it was sad, and it made me question subjectivity and my judgement of a place like this. It made me ask big questions. What makes what I want better than this? Who am I to decide how others should live? There was no room for judgement here and Karumba kicked me in the ass. Good and hard. The arrogance and inanity of merely wanting to be entertained, for Christ's sake! And for that reason, Karumba, even though it was the closest approximation of anything beyond hell I'd ever encountered, was better than any place I could have imagined.

My grandmother used to say that hell is where all the interesting people wind up, and while our attempts to investigate that side of the population of Karumba were quashed by a style of alcohol consumption that had a Jonestown kind of feel to it, what I think she meant is that in hell, nothing is whitewashed. Heaven is for scaredy-cats, for people who want answers to all the usual questions. And Karumba was for people who lived in the questions and who never expected them to be answered. Hell was more pure than heaven could possibly be. It was a nightmare, but, as David Mitchell wrote, 'Nightmares are sent by who, or what, we really are, underneath; don't forget where you are from, the nightmare tells. Don't forget your true self.'

And so, I found myself actually sad to go. We had found Karumba's charm, but there was nothing left to be done there. We finished our beers, left some money on the bar and walked slowly back to the car. And as we drove away, south and west toward Darwin, made even more distant by our detour, we did not sit on the roof of the Kingswood or perform acrobatic moves from moving car to dirt bike. We sat silently, looking out the windows, letting the hot air and dust sweep in, and we felt what it was like to be pure and true and alive.

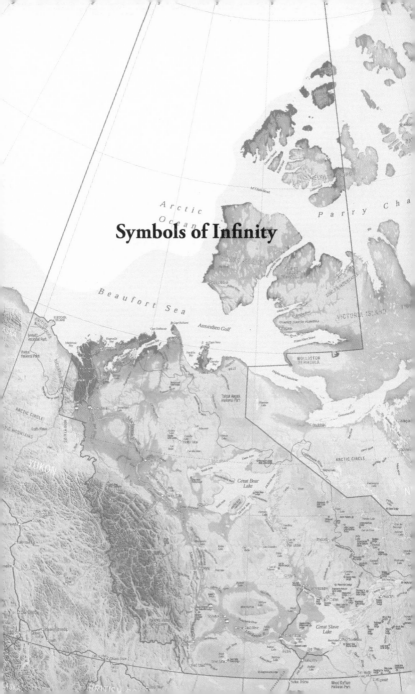

# Symbols of Infinity

YELLOWKNIFE IS SITTING ON A GOLD MINE. And I don't mean that metaphorically. A vein (and a shaft to get to it) runs right under the city.

I'm leaning against the doorway of the place where I'm staying and the ground gives a short, sharp roll like an aftershock.

'Did you feel that?' I ask the motel owner behind me.

He looks up and asks, 'What?'

'Like an earthquake,' I say.

'Oh,' he says. 'That's them blasting.' And he sighs like he's had to explain it to a million people. Which he probably has. His manner reminds me of the signs in Southeast Asian hotels forbidding the heavily pungent durian fruit in the lobby and rooms. I don't know why. Maybe something to do with feeling like you have to apologize for a completely normal part of your life to someone who exists in a completely separate loop – someone who can try to understand, but probably never will.

~

It's a Wednesday night in the middle of August, and Bryan, the friend of a friend, and I are at the Black Knight. When we walked in, his face fell and he looked sideways at me. Apologized for how quiet the place was. Later, he does the same at the Gold Range, the most notorious bar in

town. He's never seen it so low-key. He says this as someone lurches past, pushing Bryan into me, someone who
takes his half-bottle of beer to the other side of the bar and
smashes it on the stage, where a local AC/DC cover band
keeps playing. Laconically.

A woman walks in and announces that her car has been
broken into. All conversation stops; you can hear the
needle being dragged across the record Yellowknife likes
to play for tourists. People turn to me. 'This never happens
in Yellowknife,' they say over and over again. 'I have never
heard of this happening and I've lived here my whole life.'

I'm here on what's called a 'fam' trip, a sort of promo-
tional gig arranged by the government where they pay for
a journalist's expenses and show them the sights in the
hopes that what the journalist has to say will boost tour-
ism. Everyone here seems to know this. The woman whose
car was broken into is standing at the bar, already halfway
through a bottle of Kokanee, laughing.

'Oh, they didn't take anything,' she says. 'They just
smashed the little triangle window in the back and went
through all my stuff – CDs, everything – but they left it all
alone.' The people in the bar who know what I am give me
a satisfied look, like this is proof it never happens. Insert
a journalist and places are suddenly changed against their
will. They're never the way they always are when someone
with a pen and a blank notebook shows up. 'Don't put that
in your story,' they always say. 'It's not real.'

Outside the bar, green swashes of light streak overhead, and there's a band of daylight rimming the horizon.

It's 2 a.m.: difficult for me to tell if it's from the sunset or encroaching dawn.

A Dogrib man walking down the street stops in front of me. 'Hey,' he says, poking me in the shoulder, 'you're other.'

'What?'

'The Territory,' he says, looking at me. He closes his eyes and recites a litany of statistics. Five per cent Métis, six per cent Dene, three per cent Northern Cree, eighty-six per cent other. I laugh. We shake hands and he and Bryan and I walk down the rest of the block together, not saying anything. Looking up at the sky, not trying to predict where the lights will veer in the next second, or the one after that.

~

*'... it was merely (Franklin's) weird death that brought us to the Arctic for good, first in the form of search parties, and then as traders, missionaries, police, resettlement administrators, our purpose long and sharp and spiralled like a narwhal horn ... '*
– William T. Vollmann, *The Rifles*

I read Vollmann before I came here. Well, first I read Mackenzie's journals, and about Franklin's interior voyages, and then I read Vollmann, an itinerant, slightly crazed and avant-garde American writer who has spent a lot of time in the Canadian North – he even lost his eyebrows up here, and how many people can say that about a place?

I read Vollmann because I didn't want the stereotypes of the north to take over; if you're going to be navigating an arena that has been overgeneralized, you need to find out if Vollmann has written about that arena and if he has, you need to read him. Because when he writes about a place, he will show you a different angle, even if he found the pre-existing stereotypes and generalizations to be true. With Vollmann, you rotate through infinite loops of individual story – stories without beginning or end, like you just dropped in on the monologue of someone's life and have to leave before it's over. He deconstructs the stereotype so that the stereotype dissolves, becomes unimportant. Becomes insulting. As it should.

You know the stereotypes of the North: the igloos and dogsleds and tipis and polar bears and blah blah blah. The misfits, the people who like being isolated, people who've never aspired to the things southern, urban Canadians consider necessities, people who think nothing of what we'd now call a lifestyle with pioneering tendencies (and by that you know we mean chopping wood for heat, shooting an animal so that you can actually use it). It's a stereotype so rooted in the North's culture that Yellowknife's tourist brochure devotes five pages to innocently marketing this phenomenon.

I used to know a reformed heroin addict who would shoot up once a year to remind herself why she quit. 'The larger the searchlight, the larger the circumference of the unknown,' she used to say. I think of her every time I meet someone here who says, 'I came up here on a one-year contract twenty years ago.'

At the Yellowknife airport, waiting for a flight across the lake to Hay River, I'm introduced to the Speaker of the Territorial House. He's on his way to the Cook Islands (the South Pacific Cook Islands, he says) to deliver a paper on conflict of interest. He's keen to go and gives me an endearing speech which takes pendulous swings between the necessity of his being there and his surprise at being asked. We talk a bit about the NWT and how politics have changed since the formation of Nunavut. He hasn't reached any grand conclusions, he says. Some things are easier, less complicated now, but some are harder. There's less money and fewer people and agencies to allocate it to, but the distribution is different and everyone needs to adjust to it. The one thing he thinks about a lot, he says, is how, if the physical boundaries of the Northwest Territories keep changing, that change will affect the territory's identity. Will it mean a loss of its individuality, or just a shift in its character? He tilts his head and thinks about it some more.

His cellphone rings. 'Probably the Prime Minister,' he says, winking at me from under his DQ ball cap. He talks on the phone for a bit, then hangs up and tells me how he bungled his first meeting with Tony Blair by not realizing who he was. Laughing. On the way to the departure gate, we see the premier, unescorted, standing in the middle of the crowd – where everyone knows everyone and some people have come here just to see who's getting off the plane – checking messages on his cellphone.

˘

There was a guy who came up to Hay River from the States not too long ago. He slipped sideways into its small population and spent the winter with his ear cocked to an abandoned early-warning-system dish perched on the shore of Great Slave Lake. He was listening for sounds from space, looking for proof of extraterrestrial intelligence. He ran out of money. He went back home.

Hay River's claim to fame – as though in competition for a bizarre history (defenestration in Prague, for example) – is detonation:

• 1819: The North West Company accidentally blows up its entire supply of gunpowder.

• Early 1970s: First a small building, then Hay River's courthouse are blown up deliberately with sticks of dynamite. Still unsolved.

• Today: Rumours of draft dodgers, Wounded Knee Indians and arms caches of various provenances still circulate. No proof ever willingly uncovered.

˘

A friend of mine wants me to hate Hay River. An old girlfriend of his who really did a number on him was from there, and when I told him I was going, he giggled and said, 'If I give you her old address, will you throw tomatoes at her house?'

Another friend who worked up at a fish camp for four years on an island in Great Slave Lake wants me to love it. 'Everyone's a character,' he says, 'everyone's got a story.' For him, Hay River was an oasis of haze – defined relatively as a narrow strip of civilization, his escape from the camp spent almost exclusively at an 'authentic' bar called the Zoo. Don't get me wrong. He liked both places – the camp and the Zoo. He existed in both, just separately. 'If you go to the bar,' he tells me, 'try and go with someone. A woman alone will not come out of there unscarred.'

Truth is, I'm already nostalgic about Hay River, and I've only just arrived. It started with the flight over on an old DC-3 prop nicknamed the Gooney Bird, each and every one of its twenty-seven seats full, the plane making so much noise it reminded me of what flying actually means. It ends with an evening on the southern shore of Great Slave Lake, still littered with driftwood (and I mean kilometres and kilometres of whole fallen trees here) from when the ice broke up a couple of months ago.

A woman I meet traipsing over those logs, an astonishing number of them chewed to a sandglass shape by beavers, says it's too bad, that they'll have to wait till next year to see if they'll have a beach again, to see if the logs get carried away by the wind and ice, the same things that put them there. In the distance, a couple of ten-year-old girls have lit a campfire. The heat from it is rising in shimmering waves and they run around near it – over the logs, into the water, back to the fire – in their bathing suits, with sandy, tanned limbs. Nothing but the sound of small waves washing up on shore, the occasional crack from the fire, the twins laughing a few hundred metres away. I sit on a log and look out at the lake – all sky and water in front and low, pined and poplared shoreline behind me – and all I want is my childhood back. Summers on Georgian Bay, when there was nothing like video to distract us from being real.

Another woman invites me to a fish fry at her camp. Some tipis, a wall tent, old Bombadiers to take the kids out on the ice in winter. Faye grew up on the mighty Mackenzie, moving up and down the river by dogsled or moosehide canoe whenever her father, a patrolman for the parks, needed to be somewhere else. Elders – ones who are old enough, anyway – tell stories of living on the Mackenzie during the influenza epidemic at the turn of the last century. You'd see a canoe floating downriver, they say, everyone inside it dead. That's how quick it got to you. But Faye is too young to have that story to tell.

The fish is good. So is the bannock. '*Mársi cho.*' That's Slavey for *thank you.*

Faye smiles and nods. She says, 'Safe travels wherever you go, hey?'

~

Running along the edge of high cirrus cloud on the way to Fort Smith, 270 kilometres southeast of Hay River, thin, spindly spruce poke out of a 360-degree horizon of low pine, top-heavy, like probes. Again and again.

A few hours later, half an hour before Fort Smith, and twenty dusty minutes off the highway, we come to the edge of an escarpment. The pines and poplars fall away and there is a vast expanse of plain as far as the eye can see. It's a salt plain, though that's not entirely evident. Three-hundred-and-seventy kilometres long, 150 kilometres wide and one of the many anomalies of Wood Buffalo National Park that make it a World Heritage site. I've always liked the idea of trying to force mutation into a set of prerequisites that will qualify it as a mutation again. It's like watching sand fall through an hourglass: wide and free, then a brief, breathtaking moment of grains corralled into a narrow opening before they fall free again into the bottom half of the glass.

A brief explanation of what this is. Ground water and precipitation mix and the salt that gets picked up gets pushed out when it meets the granite shield – in this case, the escarpment. From above, the plain is an embroidery of isolated pockets, paint-by-number. Salt deposit here. Lush prairie grass here. River with Rapunzel-like weeds coursing through here. More salt. Some coniferous trees. Buffalo grazing peacefully, little black dots way in the distance.

Down on the plain, the sand is hard and hot underfoot. Neck-high grass on the other side of the river sways in the breeze, and the air comes at us in bursts of sweetness. The sun is blinding, the colours shocking and real. Salt collects in columns as high as my waist at the opening of a spring near the base of the escarpment. And I laugh, because I feel like I've been dropped into a hermeneutic circle as expressed in landscape. This makes sense.

'Yeah, it does,' says Anna, the biologist I'm with.

'Is Mike taking you to Grosbeak Lake tomorrow?' she asks.

I nod.

She shakes her head. 'Now, that place is just plain weird.'

The impossibly long legs of a crane (only the legs) lie perfectly splayed on mud cracked with dryness, two feathers nearby the only betrayal that it was once more than this, that it was alive.

~

Fact: Uranium in the Great Slave Lake area was mined in the early 1940s for the Manhattan Project. They loaded it on barges on the Hay and Slave rivers, where it went down the Mackenzie to the Beaufort Sea. The Northwest Territories is notorious in quiet, surprising ways.

All morning, Mike, the Parks guy who's taking me to all his favourite places, gives me the spiel that isolation here is a selling point, how the business philosophy in this part of the country is to stay small. I've been listening. We drove down Wood Buffalo's main road for two hours and didn't see anyone else but buffalo. They disappeared into the forest like ghosts – dissolved, almost. It's the height of summer and tourist season, and the campground where I'm staying in Fort Smith is half-full on the busiest week-end of the year. That means that nine sites are taken up. So, okay: it's an interesting concept, but it's inherently counter to the idea of business. I mean, the whole point of selling something is to get more people interested in what you have to sell, and then you deal with the consequ–

I look up. Anna was right. We've been hiking through forest for twenty minutes and suddenly we're at the edge of it. Grosbeak Lake. Mike is ahead of me, standing on a lake bed that hasn't seen water in a few centuries. He's quiet, which is almost more jarring than the landscape. The shore of the lake is half a mile away, and between us and it is an expanse of salt. I wish I could tell you that it was like something, but honestly, it's not like anything but itself. The sky is a blue so intense you feel like you could reach all the way to the moon, rimmed with knives of evergreen and salt so uniform and devoid of colour you think you can see the curvature of the earth. Small boulders are scattered across it, slowly being eaten away by the salt. We walk across it, stepping over delicate shards that look like ice forming, or hoarfrost, except that it's thirty above, and it's salt. It's a bit like being in the middle of a bowl of cereal just after someone's sprinkled some brown sugar on it, and looking up into an infinite sky.

Mike stands with his hands on his hips, one leg pushed out a bit further than the other. He adjusts his sunglasses and grins at the scenery. He looks back at me.

'You go to Banff, you're going to see people. You come here ... '

I bite.

~

Not much further away, Mike and I go swimming in a sinkhole. Where two sinkholes are joined, to be exact. We swim at the narrowest point, where the two strands of the symbol of infinity intersect, if you can picture it. ∞. Right there. The water is deep and clear and cool and forever changing colour, from one intensity to another. Blue. Green. Black. Mike's still grinning. I wonder if he's ever unhappy. He came up here on a two-year contract ten years ago.

~

Fort Smith is hopping. It's opening night at the South Slave Friendship Festival and a small, transient crowd has gathered at the stage in the park in the centre of town. Bands play and people just come and go, or hop up on stage with them and join in, then hop off and mill about, catching up on gossip or dipping into the old movie theatre next to the park, which is open just to sell popcorn and extra-long strawberry Twizzlers.

A woman pushes a stroller full of groceries, and a baby in there somewhere. Kids are hanging out at Liz's having a slushie. An Aboriginal man with fantastic wrinkles sits on a bench in an abandoned corner, shouting hello at anyone who happens to catch his eye, no matter how far away they are. Everyone seems happy, or at least content. The roar of the Rapids of the Drowned on Slave River fills the dead air between songs and bands. Since yesterday, someone has built an inukshuk on a slab of smooth granite that pokes out into the river. It's a big one. I stare at it for a long time.

A souped-up Honda with tinted windows and Ontario plates thumps past, leaving a wake of muffled electrobeat. Outside the Arctic Oasis Lounge, there's a dirty, scratched four-by-four with three river kayaks and a mountain bike crammed onto its roof. From Texas. A cloud of laughter floats out from the bar, then evaporates.

A guy comes up to me, tells me that if I want a ticket for the Super Shaker tomorrow night ('basically a dance at the arena where the locals drink too much'), I can't get one because it's sold out. 'But if you come with me … ' he says. Less than a minute later, he locates a ticket. Twenty-seven of them, in fact.

Later that night, I meet someone who starts a story with a deadpan face, and, 'Now, back when Moby Dick was just a minnow … ,' and fall in love with his idealism, the complete fusion of humour with consequence.

~

'And well, they like the Bingo, eh?' Jane says about her friends. She's describing the process of fish-scale painting. She takes the scales off the fish and cleans them, then makes a picture with them, scale by scale. Fish-scale artists up here say that bingo markers work just as well to paint the scales as anything else. And by golly, the colours jump out at you. They never did that with regular paint.

Jane is a craft artist. She teaches workshops on moccasin making and beading, caribou tufting, porcupine quill embroidery and so on. She says to me, 'I made a deal with my husband.' Did she ever.

They have a cabin on the trapline. Each winter they go and stay there for a couple of weeks to trap things, go other places to shoot bigger things. She's got eight or nine beaver skins nailed to boards drying out in her garage right now, just did them yesterday. But this is the deal, she tells me: 'I make him give me a pelt of every kind of animal we shoot.'

She pulls them out of hockey bags stashed in a big shed at the back of her property. Muskox. Winter caribou. Marten. Beaver. Wolf. Moose. Grizzly. Jane shows me two hides, one of them from the winter caribou, plush and soft and smooth, completely unblemished. Like a field of snow fresh after a storm, at the moment that the wind dies. Sparkling in sunshine, pure, before it has a chance to settle into the landscape's hollows. Infinity. The second is a summer hide of caribou, thinner, weaker, pockmarked with holes bored by worms – parasites that reside in the caribou's skin. 'There's not much you can do about that,' she says. It's just the way it is.

A smoke tree is a tree that grows only in arid areas. What makes it particularly distinct is that its branch system is an exact replica of its root system, the part of the tree you assume you can never see. Right then, when Jane showed me those caribou skins, swishing through the stench of beaver flesh; when I stood on the edge of the escarpment and saw those buffalo glide across the plain; on the plane flying over Great Slave Lake and standing in a sea of driftwood a few hours later, I felt like I was looking at a cross-section of a smoke tree – suspended between history and possibility, between definition and evolution. I felt housed between reflections, and I understood why we need and how we are defined not merely by places of strange and isolated beauty but by the distance between them, whether they are pinpoints or unending ribbons.

It's like what Mike said as he swam through the inter-secting lines of the sinkholes again and again. He said living up here is like living in a loop, and I bought that too, without having to ask what he meant.

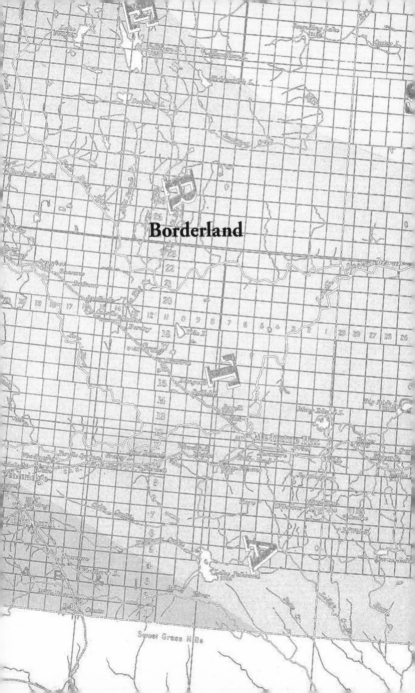

# Borderland

A COUPLE OF YOUNG GUYS BEHIND ME are talking about hockey. They're upset that Roman Turek, the Flames' regular goalie, is back – they hope Sutter trades him soon; they think that Sutter hopes so too. The wind outside is picking up. It's going a good clip now, much stronger than it was an hour ago. It's almost a tumbleweed a-tumblin' kind of wind, and if it weren't for all the cornfields around, this would be a tumbleweed a-tumblin' kind of place. The kind of bright sunlight that you only see in southern Alberta, the kind that washes everything out.

I squint out the window and watch a Department of Homeland Security officer drive my sister's car into a big shed, watch as a corrugated metal door shuts behind it. That your car?, one of the hockey guys asks me. I shake my head, tell them it's my sister's, that I borrowed it for this trip. They ask where I'm going. Minneapolis, to visit some friends, I say, And you? Salt Lake, they say, to visit some friends too and, one of the guys leans forward with his eyes all lit up, maybe catch a game. He grins. I ask them how long it'll take. They don't know – they figure between eight and twelve hours, due south from here. No speed limit in Montana. Then Idaho, then sweet Utah. I-15, all the way …

The officer drives my sister's car out and parks it. Steps out of it and the wind nearly blows the car door back onto her. A big dust cloud tornadoes across the lot and she turns away, her hair standing on end. She comes inside, brushes herself off, crooks her finger at me once she's behind the counter.

Explain your passport to me, she says. I don't understand what you were doing in all these places. She flips back and forth through it. Like Cuba.

Just travelling, I say.

In *Cuba*? she asks.

Yes, I say. There was a music festival I wanted to see.

And India? What's this India business?

I was just travelling, I say.

Why?

I'm naturally curious, I say. But she's halfway across the room before I finish, shaking her head.

Come over here, she says. She leads me into a room with a door that locks automatically behind me. Put your left index finger here, she says. Why? I ask. We're sending you back to Canada, she says. Why? I ask. We'll tell you that later. Now put your finger here.

I ask if I'm being charged or arrested for something. No, she says. It's policy. We fingerprint and photograph anyone who's denied entry. I think about a friend of mine who had his address book photocopied by police once, in lieu of an unjustified arrest, and wonder which is worse. I tell her I refuse to be fingerprinted on principle, since I've done nothing wrong, and never have, and since I'm being sent back to Canada anyway and it's not apparent why. She waves a man over and speaks to him in a low tone for about five minutes, points at the tourist visas in my passport. He nods, looks over at me.

I understand you're being uncooperative in providing us with information, he says. No, I say, I've been honest and forthright. Biometric information, he says, pointing to the small electronic pad next to him. You cannot leave without being fingerprinted and photographed, he says, and no, you do not have the right to legal representation at the U.S. border.

The hockey kids are long gone, cleared of narcotic suspicion. Heading south on I-15 with all their anticipation bubbling up in front of them.

The officer keeps pressing my finger against the touchpad. She holds it gently, picks it up and places it down, rubs the skin gingerly when it doesn't take. I can tell she has a child. And maybe if I asked, she might pause and think to herself how quickly time passes, how she always sees her son as eight, but how he's thirteen now. She asks me if I've ever cut my fingers because they can't get a good scan on either index finger. I tell her that I used to work in kitchens, that the prints probably burned off long ago. She nods, looking at her computer screen. Hold still. Clicks her mouse. The image finally takes.

She tells me I'm being sent back because I lack ties to Canada. That they need to see a bank statement, more proof of material possession – a house, say, or at least a car – and more than three changes of clothes for a one-week stay. I tell her that I've lived in Canada for thirty-five years and if that isn't a tie, I don't know what is. But that's okay, I say, I won't come back. If this is the cost of visiting the United States, I won't abide it. I will not be a part of paranoid policy.

On the Canadian side, I give the customs officer a sheet of paper with my name and file number on it. She looks at it, looks at me, a smile of empathy. Why didn't they let you in? I open my mouth, but anger comes up so quickly from my stomach that I'm seized with silence. It's okay, she says, you don't have to tell me. It just makes a long day longer. And she tells me I can go.

I drive north, the windshield all sun and sky and brown cornfields, a long sword of horizon. It's half an hour before I can breathe, I mean really breathe, take a breath that reminds me of where I am. All that space and air around me and half an hour goes by before the fingers wrapped around my throat loosen, fingers with unscannable tips, just like the ones I have wrapped around the steering wheel of my sister's car.

I AM OVERSEAS, talking to some people. It isn't important where or with whom. A group of young men, say, in one of those ubiquitous plazas, a cluster of hopeful girls in scarves hovering an awkward distance behind them. The sun is shining. The plaza is busy. There is a light breeze. And then it begins, like it always does.

*Where are you from?*, they ask. *Canada,* I say. *Oh.* They nod and say, *America.*

*No, Canada.*

*Yes, yes,* they say, looking at each other. (*Isn't Canada ... ?*) One of them nods at the others. *Yes, America,* they all say. They shrug and they are certain America and Canada are the same thing.

They are not the same thing. Not by a long shot.

Now, I guarantee you that this is not going where you think it is. This is not about patriotism. No, this is about opportunity, about capitalism. And about mediocrity.

~

I'm on the SeaBus going from Lonsdale Quay to downtown Vancouver. There are two couples sitting in front of me, grey-haired, clutching things. Bags. Canes. Arms. One couple grabs the other couple's arms and points excitedly at the Harbour Centre, a concrete block maybe thirty storeys high. Barely a landmark. 'This place is exciting,' one woman says to the other, 'because it has a restaurant that revolves.' The other couple's eyes widen. As though nothing beyond that could ever impress them, or be accessible to them, as though the newer world is so entirely composed of separate things – of glass and skyscrapers and mobile phones and speed – and requires such a leap of understanding from what they already know, that there is no chance to evolve into it.

I watch them, bemused. The back page of a past issue of the *New Yorker* comes to mind. It is a mock application, printed just after Bush reclaimed the White House, to immigrate to Canada. Multiple choice. *I want to come and live in Canada because: A. I missed out on the fifties.*

I've spent a fair amount of time in America. Annual summer trips to Maine as a kid. Six months in San Francisco in my mid-twenties. Month-long residencies, internships, apprenticeships. Why? Because there were things there that were not available in Canada. At least not without great effort, experience, expense, justification. It was easier to do them in America.

America has changed me. Yes it has. Here's how. One word. You know what that word is, don't you? Yes, you do, because you're Canadian. It's not even a word, you say, it's a name. That's right.

Gatsby.

All those green lights blinking away across the sound, all that unfettered wealth and possibility. All that *excellence*.

∞

⌣

I get off the SeaBus and walk toward the west end. Robson Street teems with GAPs and Old Navys. Starbucks on opposite corners. But for the people on the street saying *sooth* and *aboot* instead of *sowth* and *abowt*, you'd never know you were in Canada. You don't need to. You can spend greenbacks here as though they're local currency.

I'm in town for dinner with an American. We're meeting at the Fairmont in an hour. Before that, I'm meeting a friend. He has a punk rock band, better than most, but he struggles. I asked him once if he'd considered trying to tap into the American market, strategically placing his CDs at various radio stations in New York, L.A., San Francisco. He just looked at me. Canadians will understand the impossibility of this kind of thinking. Americans will not. When my cousin's first mainstream book was published, American friends simply said to her, 'Well, you have to get on Oprah.' Like it was a matter of a phone call, not a change in ideology. As though success were necessitated by (association with) celebrity. I was not suggesting this to the punk rocker. But survival – not even success – in Canada does necessitate recognition outside of the country. No matter how small. And the not-so-small resentment of it. It is an unspoken thing between us now. Like Canadian films in the 'foreign' section at the video store. Or the automatic loading of American spellings in English computer dictionaries. Center. (Centre.) Gray. (Grey.) Neighbor. (Neighbour.) Yard. (Metre.)

I'm waiting to cross the street by the art gallery. It's dusk and it's busy. Skater kids are riding stairs and handrails, people are coming from or going to dinner. There is traffic. Cabs. Buses. A couple of obscenely long suv limos. One of the skater kids flicks a finger at a limo but doesn't say or shout anything. That is enough. Yes, you *are* in Canada, where even rebelliousness is polite, considerate, safe.

Across the street from the art gallery is a glass building. A large chain bookstore occupies the bottom two levels and it is lit up so you can see everyone inside perusing best-sellers, flipping through ads in magazines, sipping large coffees. The building reminds me of a Rubik's cube with all its windows and colours lined up in rows and the inter-changeability of the squares. The name of the company on the roof is ∞. No words. Just the symbol.

Across the street, attached to the south side of the gallery, is a lit banner for an exhibition of a collection of photographs. The photo on the banner is remarkable. It was taken from the roof of a building, looking down past the facade of another building, where a soldier is erecting a

∞

Soviet flag, lunging to get it in right, over a city of smoke and rubble. It looks a hundred years old. Grainy. Gritty. Substantial.

I stand at that intersection for a long time, looking back and forth between the two. It feels a bit surreal. I wonder what made ∞ possible. Surely not that photo. But yes, it did. It's 1945. The fall of Berlin. It seems to me that ∞ has no memory, that the photo has too much of it. 'Berlin,' a friend who had lived there once told me, 'is a city suffering from an overdose of history.' And here we are, Canada, standing on the corner, looking up at both ∞ and history, burdened with the knowledge of that conflict. Between destruction and utopia. Between Europe and America, aware of the differences like America could never afford to be. It's much easier to get people to participate in a system without baggage, by ignoring things like differences, turning inwards. I'm not envious of it, but I do think Canadians are in a unique position to see it and to apply the past to the present and future.

We wouldn't survive if we remembered everything. The way information is lost is as important as the way it is retained. Take dentures, for instance. Think about what they used to be made of. Real teeth. From dead people, or people who didn't need them anymore. It makes sense when you think of it, but it doesn't even occur to us now that there wasn't always some artificial material used to make them. 'False teeth.' That's what we grew up calling them. The manufacture of something synthetic to replace the real. Berlin was only sixty years ago. And yet it seems impossible to absorb, comprehend, in a meaningful way. Because now we have ∞. And skyscrapers and mobile phones. And really not that much of substance to worry about, though we spend a lot of time trying to convince ourselves that we do.

A breeze ripples through the banner. It's nearly dark now. I'm going to be late for that dinner. I wait for the light to blink green and cross the street, skateboards *click-clack, click-clack*ing, noises colliding in the air behind me.

I spent October 2001 and July 2002 in Minnesota. Crossed over the Mississippi into Wisconsin a couple of times to visit a friend of a friend, but mostly stayed near the Twin Cities. I like the Twin Cities. They've got something –

∞

I think it's guts, but understated. It's still got Gatsby, but with a taste of Canada. Perhaps that's why I feel like I understand it.

Let me tell you about the Gatsby I found there.

October 2001. You can imagine. America's naïveté – a naïveté about the rest of the world that was once not only forgivable but *important*, essential, because it seemed as though America could not be great without it – was gone. There was a sense that possibility was being forced out of a small crack, that the luxury and vastness of it had been condensed by the sudden filling of that space by aggression, that there were few Americans (and at least one Canadian) with their lips to that small crack, trying to draw it into themselves before it was gone. A poem of W. G. Sebald's goes:

*It is*

*as though I lay*
*under a low*
*sky and breathed*
*through a needle's eye.*

Like that.

And yet ... and yet. This was when and where I discovered what I do for a living now. It is an obscure profession. Old-fashioned letterpress printing. Like Gutenberg. I stumbled into a building that had vertically integrated all of the aspects of this profession and made a public space for it. It was a permissive atmosphere that encouraged exploration, redefinition of paradigms with equipment that was no longer easy to find. Freedom. Excellence.

I cast everything aside. I did not sleep for days.

This was not Canada.

When I went back home I felt, as I always do, like my country had pulled me aside as soon as I'd stepped back across the border and said, Look now, you can't do that kind of stuff here. Be realistic about it. Possibility is not as possible as it seems. Optimism tempered. And so we slip into mediocrity.

I was determined not to be tempered. I arranged for an apprenticeship – in America. Because that seemed the natural place to take a plunge. I felt that if I did one in Canada, I might decide not to go ahead with this – that I would allow the difficulties of the profession, the reality of it, to stop me.

July 2002. The apprenticeship. The general atmosphere in America was almost raw, like there was no longer a translucency to opportunity – that it had turned into pure greed, the illusion had been deliberately stripped away by the institution of consumerism (which is, after all, a form of opportunity). A brazen 'fuck you.' *You don't like capitalism? We'll show you capitalism. Just watch us.*

And yet, amidst all that, there were people continuing in their obscure professions, doing excellent things with a quiet determination and a wilful ignorance of the ugly side of opportunity. And why shouldn't they, after all? It was an interesting collision. The quality of both obscurity and consumerism seemed dependent on that collision. But in Canada we would have hesitated, faltered, reconsidered. Been *sensible*. In America? No way.

That's Gatsby. I can't think of a Canadian Gatsby. Trudeau had some Gatsby in him, but half the country hated him and I don't know a single person in America who hates Gatsby.

Maybe Gretzky. That's the other thing people say when you tell them you're from Canada. *Oh! Hock-eeeyyy! Gretzkyyyy!* And their eyes light up. Yeah, maybe him. But he lives in America now. Because he can.

There was a guy in high school, John Izumi, who was a great pitcher. His marks were not as great as how his body twisted on the mound when he threw the ball. He didn't qualify for any Canadian universities, and there were no such things as sports scholarships here. He wound up getting a baseball scholarship to Purdue. Going south was the only way he'd get a post-secondary education – his own country couldn't accommodate him, had no vision for him. There was another guy, a closer friend than Johnny I, a filmmaker now. He says he has to live in New York to do what he wants to do. We all know people like this. Can you picture it the other way around?

~

There's a thirty-foot boat near where I live, lying on its side halfway up a mountain. It lies next to a bulldozer, like there's some plan for it – at least that's what I used to think. But I've given up on that theory after three years of seeing it there.

Now I like to think that this sideways boat is a maze. Of possibility. In the quantum sense. It exists as a boat only when we look at it as a boat, or within the paradigm of a boat: a series of particles. Only when we are conscious of it. You look at it, you see a boat lying on its side. You bring your experiences of boats lying on their sides (or other things) into the picture. You determine that this thing must be useless, or too damaged to be where it should be, in the water. But imagine. You look away, you erase the boat from your memory and vision and you look back and all you can see are waves of possibility. The boat has become invisible. What is there now is physically intangible, but emotionally present. Where ideas are more real than the physical. It's this intangibility that moves inertness into action, chaos into form. It's this uncertainty that is so necessary to the precise.

The boat, after all, is just a boat. Lying on its side. Useless particles.

—

I was on my way back to America for a visit. The barrenness (physical, intellectual) of western Canada in winter had gotten to me so I planned a week-long visit to the Twin Cities to see friends, to re-inject some of that possibility, bring some of it back with me.

At the border, I was stopped in my tracks. Forbidden. I was bemused at first, then confused, then deliberately uncooperative. I had never done anything wrong in my life (officially), yet I was brought into a locked room and

∞

my fingerprints and photograph were taken before I was told why I wasn't being allowed to visit my friends, the Midwest, all that possibility. 'You lack ties in Canada,' the Department of Homeland Security said. 'It will be difficult for you to visit America again.' Then I got angry.

This was not possibility.

American friends responded with disgust, and countered with stories of extra questioning at the Canadian border, of suspicious border guards who eventually let them through. It is not the same thing. It is not the same as government policy forcing someone to give fingerprints and a photograph despite being denied entry, and before being told why.

~

Near where I live, an old railway yard is being dismantled. This is happening very slowly, almost unnoticeably, in the sense that I never see people working on the dismantling. Things just disappear.

First, the old cars go. Cars from the twenties and thirties, some still in fine shape, some of which had been used by squatters, the homeless.

Then there are fewer trains coming through. The whistle and clack that brought comfort at midnight now mute.

I used to stand at the tracks, near a bridge, when a train went past, feeling the rumble in my feet,

grain cars
livestock cars
propane cars
cars of excess height
hazardous materials cars
empty cars
car cars
coal cars (coal cars!)
no caboose

grinning at the largeness of it all. The machinery. A *national* railway. Transport. Thousands and thousands of kilometres. The thickness of the wheels.

Sometimes I stood under the bridge as the train passed overhead, touching a trestle to feel it shake and give, letting the debris between the ties loosened by its weight settle on my head. If the landscape was sufficiently abandoned and the train was stopped, I'd climb up the ladder at the edge of one of the open cars, peer over and look inside. Sulphur. Scrap metal. Cut-up beef bones. Never the same thing twice. At the base of the grain cars, by the couplings, spilled grain had always sprouted into carpets of lush grass, so that from the top it looked as though the cars were partially submerged in a rich lawn or golf course green. And I would look down the track twisting endlessly toward the horizon and think, *This is the possibility Canada was built on.*

Waves to particles. Back to waves. The railway yard disappears in the space of about six weeks. Suddenly, unceremoniously, after more than a century of physically

∞

connecting this vast, sparsely populated country, the train is just an idea again.

~

This American. It's a bit of a long story. He and I have never met. He's responsible for my being obsessed with what I do, for getting me into this mess. He was the brains behind that building I walked into, the one that changed my life. I found out that he was going to be in Vancouver, got in touch with him, said, 'I want to buy you a drink to say thanks.' He said, 'You can buy me a drink. Then we can go to dinner.' He had never been to Vancouver before and rumo(u)r had it he was a connoisseur of fine cuisine, so I suggested a few places to match his palate. He ignored them. Found out what the most expensive French restaurant in town was and made a reservation there. My eyes widened when he emailed me the details. I went to the closet to see if I had a pair of heels.

I trip into the Fairmont – which used to be the Hotel Vancouver, which used to be owned by Canadian Pacific Railway, which used to be one in a series of hotels that held this country together – and he is at the bar, swirling three olives in a martini. Licking the stick. It's dark out now, and we watch red-and-white blurs of light streak past through huge new plate-glass windows. We have a drink and I tell him why I owe it to him. He keeps telling me my voice is soft and we finish our drinks and then we head to the restaurant.

He orders champagne, then asks if a bottle and a half of wine with dinner will be too much. 'Yes,' I say softly. He announces to everyone – the hostess, the waiters, the sommelier – that he is from America and that we have never met. Confidence. His stories are big and fabulous – and there is an attraction. The way he thinks. On such a large scale. Inertness into action. Chaos into form. And my voice so soft. Me, the lightweight, but he seems not to mind. He continues to tell me stories. Meeting Havel at Prague Castle. The things he did for Lauren Bacall. Why he is good at what he does and what needs to be done. Immediately. No hesitation. He asks me, 'Where are you ten years from now?' A question I have never asked myself, nor which I have ever been asked in Canada. One that would have been asked sooner if I'd spent more time in America.

He reminds me of the possibility that is no longer so easily available. He makes me taste it again, and realize what I am giving up, what has been denied. 'But it's ironic, don't you think,' I say to him, 'that this place of possibility should begin to be unreasonably selective?' It means that possibility may soon ebb.

Here, we think, *Let someone else take the risks*. Good enough is our best. Content to be beholden to those who do the best for us, so we don't have to put all that work into getting there and defending it. There are days when Canada feels like what Havel describes as a totalitarian ideology, 'a veil behind which human beings can hide their own fallen existence, their trivialization, and their adaptation to the status quo.' The mediocrity is the instrument

∞

of its discipline. A speedometer that goes to 210, but never gets used above sixty. (Kilometres.)

Another part of that *New Yorker* application for immigration comes to mind when the American orders two extra appetizers for each of us: *'if you do come here to live, we wonder if you'd be willing to "tone it down" a bit.'*

~

The halibut is a fish that frequents the waters around here. It begins its life by swimming upright in shallow water, but gradually sinks down into deep water, lying on its side with both eyes moving to the same side of the head.

After being indirectly and almost unintentionally bombarded by another country, one becomes irresolute, mute. A bottom-feeder. Content to lie on our sides and let our eyes move to accommodate our listlessness. An essay I read the other day described contemporary American culture as 'a system so pervasive that it relieves its participants of the responsibility to object, and the ability to imagine why they would ever do so.' They do not understand how Canadians could be so listless. On the other hand, there's no need to. We don't affect them in the least.

The other day I was set upon by a dog. Innate reaction to threat of security treats aggression with aggression. Or at least the threat of aggression. The raising of a hand, say. Sometimes being nice or charitable doesn't work. The barking, snarling, lunging, snapping dog is difficult to ignore. You can't let it walk all over you. At some point you have to deal with it. After hesitating, I raised my hand. It made things worse. I got bitten, just above my ankle. It felt unnatural to me, raising the hand. I am always reluctant to flee, but threatening to hit felt wrong too. The metaphor is obvious, but I don't know what conclusions to draw from it.

~

There is an attraction to a point. So much can be said in one movement. Or the lack of it.

I'd kiss him back, if there was a kiss. But there is no kiss. That he is a fetishist becomes obvious. To occupy the *idea* of something, not the person attached to it. Being with him would require a forgiveness not many of us possess.

All I had wanted to do was buy him a drink and say thanks. I have to be honest. True to Canadian style, I let him lead me into this situation.

And now look at this. The danger is apparent. *Yes, I will sleep with you. Or the idea of you. (But at what cost to me?)*

There is no attempt to seduce. Think allowing missiles to use Canadian airspace. Think NAFTA. Think fingerprints and photographs at the border. He simply lets me know what he is going to do.

Between the main course and the cheese plate, before dessert, he looks at me, leans down past the table, takes my ankle in his hand and slips off my shoe. The room falls silent, staring. He holds my gaze, holds my foot at the Achilles tendon with one hand, runs his other hand over the front of it, his index finger tracing the grooves between my toes; stares at me for a couple of minutes. Just as I am about to shout, *Okay, okay, I'll give you whatever it is*

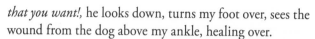

*that you want!,* he looks down, turns my foot over, sees the wound from the dog above my ankle, healing over.

I drove past the boat today, on my way down here. There was a crane lifting it from where it had lain. There was noise and there were men operating levers, standing by, watching. Pointing, shouting. The boat was lifted. It swung around toward me slightly when the keel left the ground. The side it had been lying on was crumpled, but held together by the fibreglass. Have you ever seen a crushed bone under unbroken skin? Like that. You poke it and the whole thing gives unexpectedly, its physical shell starting to disintegrate. Tomorrow it will be gone.

He runs his fingers over the wound. (210. ∞.) A woman in the restaurant gasps, the sommelier starts forward. (Sixty. Berlin.) It's still tender. In fact, it almost hurts more now than it did when it happened. But I don't pull my foot back. Ever notice how, when a scar is healed, everything that touches it feels thin? Lacking depth and texture? The vibration of a finger stops at the surface. But this, this I feel down to the bone. Like I felt possibility in America. I want him to touch it, to feel the raised pink skin, the bit of hard blood still in some spots, hotter than the unscarred skin next to it. I want him to see the natural pattern of ivory in flesh, like teeth in a ripe peach.

It is the only thing I can offer him.

'She realized how rare it was to see what sta
you, what a novelty of basic sensation in the
life of the city – to look across a measured sp
be undistracted by signs and streetlights and t
scaffolding, by your own bespattered mind, sor
data, and by the energy that hurrying people
lunch crowds and buses and bike messengers, al
consciousness powering down the flumes of Manh
so that it becomes impossible to see across a street
the turquoise tiles of some terra-cotta façade, a win
beast carved above the lintel.'

– Don DeLillo, *Underwo*

IT'S A CRAPSHOOT, always is. Nothing anyone can do about it. At least, that's what we tell ourselves.

In between you take a few trips, see some other places. You find yourself in Thailand, say, or Mexico. You get off the beaten track, either by choice or by error. You come into a town – the size doesn't matter, it's a town just like Owen Sound is, or Estevan, Bariloche or Ratnapura. You see some kids running around in the dirt, barefoot, playing with a deflated ball, or rocks and a piece of string. You stand and you watch them and you remember your own childhood and what you had. Less than kids today, but more than rocks and a piece of string. You remember how every year your mother made you give away the toys you were too old for and the ones you didn't want anymore. You can't remember whether you were a happy child or not. That detail seemed irrelevant until now.

You watch these kids and you don't see their emotional state – you see the rock and the string, the deflated ball, and what starts deep in the stomach as pity taps upward into your brain. *I'm so lucky,* you think. To have been born in a prosperous place. To have had so many toys. You think.

That pity won't stay there. It will mutate with the ferocity of a virus into guilt and shame. When you go home you will go to a dinner party and tell your closest friends about the rock and string, the deflated ball: the one moment

*Saudade*

that stuck with you more than any other. They will shake their heads and, trying to match your empathy with their own, they will say it too. *We are so lucky.* Perhaps one will recommend a therapist, as though you are the victim of something. Pass the Prosecco, please. Another lamb popsicle? Delicious. Yes, we are so lucky. As if feeling lucky (or expressing that we feel lucky) exonerates us, makes us less complicit.

You will not remember that you didn't notice whether those kids were happy or not.

It's not as simple as all that, of course. Never is. Especially in the 'post-moral age' we seem to occupy now. You didn't ask any questions while you were there, didn't spend any time with those kids. It didn't even occur to you not to jump to conclusions, that these kids might actually go to a school as good as you did, become intelligent people or have enough clothes or a real crack at a good life, because you saw the rock and the string and their bare feet and you made assumptions. That's where that deep-in-the-stomach pity came from – those assumptions (just like the ones they made about you).

It's messy.

It's disingenuous to think that way. On both sides. You know that, so you travel more, farther, longer, deeper. You think how you see things will change, and to a certain degree it does. You begin to talk to people, you begin to ask questions, you accept invitations into homes and see

152 •

how they live. But everywhere you go there is the rock and the string. It always appears somewhere. Nothing will eradicate it. The situation has not changed. Your acceptance of it has. You come to see it in a way that stems from the exoneration, bordering on denial, now. These people are happy, you think. Material possessions don't matter to them. It's a cultural thing. *I really* am *lucky. And nothing I do can help these people in the long term.* Completely washing over the real issues, which are greed, compensation, humility.

It's the way it is. Nothing can be done. Simple. If it ain't broke, don't fix it, right?

My obsession with an old-fashioned way of living began before my memory does.

My parents bought a piece of cottage property in a place unattractive to most people. It was near the northeastern edge of Algonquin, on top of a hill overlooking a quiet highway. Not near a lake. Beset by beavers. Enough black-flies in summer to permanently bruise the sky. An old long-ago-abandoned house at the top of the hill, its roof cleaved nearly to the ground so that the staircase to the second floor almost punched a hole through it. Nothing virtuous about the property except the quiet. But to two Europeans, the idea of that kind of space – enough land for it to be a challenge to see another human – must have been worth a figure well beyond the asking price. I understand this because I live in Europe now and my nostalgia for space is acute.

They bought a build-it-yourself garage to serve as a cabin and put it up in a summer with the rest of the family's help, a few hundred feet away from the cleaved house, in front of a small, disused barn. A well went in, and holes for the crapper were dug, but no electricity, no phone, were ever wanted. The plumbing stayed outdoors and a pot-bellied stove was installed for heat. It was a one-room cabin where we had to melt snow for water in winter, where the hiss of a Coleman lantern was the only sound after the sun went down and dinner was cleared away. That and the clack of Scrabble tiles or the slow turning of pages on the books in four different sets of hands. To them, it was heaven. To me, it was the sound, if not of happiness, of a contentedness that comes from entire days spent out in the cold, walking and working, followed by a meal made on top of a fire and room to think.

Parts of us will always live in the past. I can still smell that cabin, though I have not been there in twenty years, and have smelled it again when I've walked into similarly unlit, unplumbed, wood-heated places in other parts of the world, though those too are on the decline: when the Americans invaded 'poverty-ridden' Kabul and pictures of a city with lights and televisions blazing and streets jammed with local trucks were shown, I remember being surprised at the universal availability of gas and electricity and thinking that my idea of poverty needed to be updated. It's stupid to equate electricity, media and fuel with wealth, but this is how my past betrays me – it was so thirty years ago, and when I see or am in a place where someone's complaining that things cannot get any worse while they stand under a functioning light bulb and cook on a gas stove, I'm (unreasonably) inclined to disagree. Michael Ignatieff said that 'we learn how much is enough by learning what it is like to have less than enough,' but our memories are short.

~

Imagine you're living in a city of a million people. A city the size of Calgary, say, or one-third the size of Montreal. It's a wonderful city, with vivacity and architecture of an ideologically specific era, with farmer's markets and concerts and universities and a good sense of community. It's a city that has been historically important, and continues to be.

Now imagine there's a democratically elected government, but no running water or electricity is provided by them. These things are not deliberately held back, you understand, but the city's infrastructure has collapsed, and there's no money to fix it. In the meantime, the resourcefulness of the citizens has lessened the urgency of the problem – the situation has become accepted, anyway. Classes at the university stop when it gets too cold – usually from December to February – because there's no money to heat the rooms. Across the city, water and electricity are simply things citizens need to secure for themselves.

There are the public baths, which are not large enough to meet the needs of a million-strong population but which self-monitor by charging an admission equivalent to an average day's wage – for those lucky enough to have a job. The baths are never crowded. For drinking and cooking water there are public taps, and if you're a resident of said city, you bring your empty pails and found pop bottles to it. You line up for half an hour or an hour, you fill them, you somehow get it all back to your apartment a few blocks away. This will be your water for the day. For eating, for washing, for drinking and cleaning.

When you get home, you discover that the electricity is on. You rush around with your vacuum cleaner and you put four pots on the stove, filling them with different things to cook; you listen to the radio even though you don't feel like it, just to take advantage of the power because you don't know how long it will last. Your electricity, like almost everyone else's in the city, is jury-rigged to the subway. If you want electricity in this city, you can either pay high prices for unreliable service that can cut out for days on end, or you can find a piece of wire to string from your apartment to the complex, makeshift grid above. In this city, apartments that are closest to the subway and its overhead electrical grid are in high demand, because when the power goes out (and it is out more often than it is on), the subway grid is the first one to be restored. The farther away you are, the more sub-grids the power has to go through to get to your single, beaten wire (which you scavenged from an abandoned yogurt factory), and the less likely it is to be consistent or at all operational. When you're lucky, you'll have electricity for four hours in a day. When you're really lucky, those four hours will be consecutive. Otherwise, it's candles, if you happen to find some

– if you have something to trade for them. No batteries: too rare, too pricey. If you have that kind of currency, you spend it on flour or wool or meat. But you will have stars. Stars that are much closer than has become our habit to see.

This was the post-Soviet reality of a city like Tbilisi, the capital of the Republic of Georgia, just before the millennium, after nearly ten years of independence, when a market system was dropped in after seventy years of communist occupation and rule. It's Georgia's most important city, and problems of infrastructure that beset the whole country were both amplified and muted here. Amplified because of the density of population, muted because there was more hope in Tbilisi than in rural Georgia. More of a chance (and urgency) that things would be fixed.

There, water and electricity were simultaneously a privilege and a necessity. There's a way to survive without regular access to convenience, but when one actively chooses to go without it, the choice creates an undeniable charm (mostly because one can decide to renege when the reality and consequences of that choice become too difficult to manage). When one simply has to live without it, is *forced* to, there is no charm. Your energy goes into securing those things in a perfect example of Maslovian needs. It's here, after seeing the woman who owns the room you – a Western tourist in Tbilisi – are staying in walk across a field to a square and line up to fill the bottles and pails of water you consumed that you realize that choice *is* privilege. Choice is freedom, and neither privilege nor freedom is a right or an entitlement. It's here, as you run down the stairs of the building you're staying in and across the field to help the woman replenish and bring back the water you took, that you realize how despicable we the chosen privileged are, and you ask yourself exactly how is it that we have become this way? And why do we refuse to change?

You stand in the middle of the prairie in Alberta, a prairie with furiously churning windmills and oil pumps, their energy arrowing toward Calgary, Edmonton, Fort Mac. Their purpose seems abstract. You just flick the switch and you have heat, power – what you need. In Tbilisi you look up, straight up, into the sky, and all you see are wires of different thicknesses, all scavenged from some lesser purpose, connected by a few loops around longer wires, which are in turn connected to larger ones. Your picture of an electrical grid could not be more clear.

As our populations shift away from the instinctual, nature-based survival of the past and toward the economy-based system of urban areas, electricity has nearly become a right, and for all of the good it has done – allowing children to do their schoolwork at home each night when before they had to sit under a streetlamp, for example – we, the privileged, have chosen to 'progress' beyond the nostalgia of living without it. We've forgotten the hiss of the lantern and the clack of Scrabble pieces, or the snap of playing cards, the silent turning of pages. We've forgotten what it means to have, and to have not.

~

I wanted to go to Cuba before Castro died. I was intrigued by (and the one-room cabin part of me was attracted to) an active communist (or at least radically socialist) system. But when I got there, I found that the communist part was relative; concessions had been made in the interest of survival. In Cuba, appliances – hairdryers, dishwashers, blenders, microwaves, breadmakers, deep fryers, large, modern televisions – being luxuries, are not subsidized by the government, while nearly everything else is. They cost real money, payable only in U.S. dollars at the same prices as North Americans would pay at home. Castro's logic is obvious: the official daily rate of pay is about what North Americans pay for an apple, therefore appliances – things deemed luxuries – are simply unattainable. To buy them, you not only have to have the money, but you have to have, or know someone who has, U.S. dollars. In spite of this, they have become a sort of false status symbol and are widely and implausibly present in nearly every home, no matter how poor its inhabitants.

For a number of reasons, mostly stemming from that one-room cabin, I've arranged my life so that I own as little as possible (by Western standards, anyway); these are very personal choices and I don't hold myself up as an example. Further, I don't wish to deny anyone what they want, but it's difficult for me to reconcile abject poverty with the ownership of these things, or to understand how so much want could justify the spending of one's entire income on appliances that, in my opinion, one can largely live without. But then, I come from a place where a market economy actively and dishonestly fuses 'want' and 'need' for profit, and for its survival. The irrational desire for those things depresses me; I equate appliances – especially television – with boxes both metaphorical and physical, the ones we start to think in when we watch too much of it, the ones we never leave when television becomes our company, our social network.

But it's the television that revealed the sort of democracy that exists in Cuba: the sight of passersby peering into the open windows of people's living rooms to watch what was on television if they happened not to have one themselves, or happened not to be close to home if they did – crowds gathering on the street watching the news, sports, one of Castro's speeches, through someone else's open window.

Saudade

They usually didn't know the person whose television they were watching, but the owners never complained. Gathering at windows and peering in is something that's frequently done in Cuba, as often with music (live or recorded) and conversations as with television, and it provided a bit of consolation in that it seemed to make watching television more of a choice, or at least a less claustrophobic and less passive act than sitting alone inside the box looking at the box. Perhaps it seemed that way because it was easier to walk away, easier to be distracted by something more interesting happening on the street than inside, or easier to start a discussion with someone standing at the window than keeping TV-watching an introverted experience.

One evening as I walked through Santiago de Cuba, the entire evening air was lit with a blue glare. It seemed as though all the televisions in that city of half a million were on. The streets were full of people lounging at living room windows and, since there was only one channel available, the same dialogue spilled out from the open windows and reverberated through the narrow streets as I walked past, as if over a loudspeaker. There was an old film on, a Spanish one in black and white – I'm not sure which – with the same halting delivery of lines as *Casablanca*. I wandered through the streets, surrounded by the dialogue no matter where I went, turning left, right, walking down a side street and seeing the snap of colour change on onlookers' faces when the scenes changed, feeling an actor's voice booming out of the windows, turning a corner and hearing the response. *'Te quieras mi?' 'Si, si, mi amor!'* It was as though I was literally walking through the film, dialogue coming at me from all sides. Where I live it's more common now to see the blue glare of the screen reflecting off someone's walls or windows in empty streets after dark than it is to see people outside, talking over the fence, going for a walk, or kids squeezing in one last minute in the yard before being called in for the night. The cabin often comes to mind when I notice the loneliness of our streets now – it had no television or even battery-operated radio, no houses nearby that blue glares could come from, the only reflection a reflection of the half-full light from stars, which were more often a carpet than scattered points in the sky. It was isolated and lonely, but justifiably so, and that dissolved the piercing quality that loneliness in a more populated area has, made it manageable if only because it was logical, and fit.

I walked to the edge of the city and climbed a hill and I stood there alone, looking at the stars, and wondered why I was the only one there. I wondered if it was fair to blame television for providing us with such a sheltered experience that even looking at stars isn't appealing anymore. Never mind appealing – it doesn't even occur to us. It requires effort. It's not at all apparent that there is anything going on up there in the sky; there is too much silence.

A lack of noise can be frightening: the ringing in the ears that happened at the cottage, or when camping in the open is noisier than the white noise of a city. I like silence, and at the cabin I used to lie awake listening, counting the minutes between one last ember cracking and the next noise – the rustle of a vole dashing over a leaf or a bug bouncing off a pane of glass – thrilled when I lost count.

I've heard that the northern lights make a noise, but I imagine you have to be attuned to silence to hear it.

My father sold the one-room, unlit, unplumbed, wood-stove-heated cabin, and all its silences, in the early nineties. He had a couple of offers but took the lowest one to sell it to some Mennonites who promised to keep it unlit, unplumbed, heated with wood and silent. And I, for better or worse, have that root in me still, partly born of regret, partly born of the past, and have tried to live in similar places since. To be fair and honest, though, it's not only a desire motivated by sadness and history, but an instinctual need for honest, self-sufficient living. And penance. For being so lucky.

Jim Harrison wrote that 'fate has never ladled out hardship very evenly,' and that 'this frequently trips our often infantile sense of justice.' I use the word *lucky* – we all do in this context – but perhaps I mean *accidental*.

We're on a shitty, shitty road, Doug and I, our bicycles loaded down, heading north toward the Russian border. It's early morning. I'm nauseous. When I mention that to the woman who let us stay in her home, she grabs my arm and smiles in a way that utterly betrays her hope: that though I'm too old to be childless in her opinion, almost too old to even bother trying, she'll make an exception. A child will save me from this kind of life I am leading – scouring the world on a bicycle with a boyfriend, not a husband, away from my family. It is, she thinks, almost too late for me to settle down – I should have done it a long time ago. I'm almost too old to be saved. I'm twenty-nine.

I'm twenty-nine and we're in northern Georgia, where the Svans have vigorously and infamously defended their territory for well over a thousand years. It's early morning and the road is dead quiet. We can serpentine our way

around the potholes and crevasses without worry. Most of Georgia is like this (or was at the time). No cars. No money to buy them, or no money to buy gas and run the one that sits abandoned by your house. Gas sold in jars by the side of the road for those trips that cannot be walked, where a car is essential. There aren't too many of those. Most often we have the road to ourselves.

We're tired. Not altogether with it. I'm nauseous (but not pregnant). We have some difficulty finding the road out of town, but eventually we do and begin to ride north. A few kilometres outside of town, just as I'm starting to come around, we round a corner on a downhill and I look up and see a guy with a black wool cap pulled down over his face walk out of some hazelnut bushes at the bottom of the hill in front of us. Doug, ahead of me, hasn't seen him yet, but there's no turning around, there's no stopping this: I hear the *clickclick* of the man loading a rifle and see another man with a black wool cap pulled down over his face come out of the bushes with a Kalashnikov.

We stop pedalling.

The first guy starts yelling at us – he has his rifle cocked and aimed at us, finger on the trigger, bullet in the chamber, and he yells and yells. Doug puts his arms up and I get off the bike and start opening the bag where some of our money is. I note the instinctive nature of what I am doing.

We have USD$3,000 in cash – traveller's cheques and credit cards being useless in this part of the world – and we usually have it spread around, but I start to sweat when I open the bag and see that somehow I've got all of it in one place. The first guy shouts again and I look up, see Doug hand over his neck pouch. The guy grabs it, roots through it, takes all the local money and change, carefully puts the Visa card and passport back in and hands it to Doug.

They're not paying any attention to me. I slowly close the bag. Leave the money inside. When confronted with an emergency, all moral principles are suspended. I note the guilt that begins to creep up.

The second guy starts shouting at Doug – they want a video camera. We honestly don't have one, but they don't believe us and cock their Kalashnikovs at us. Doug pulls out his point-and-shoot Kodak and hands it over. They look nervously up and down the road. It's the time of day when people start to travel and someone's bound to be coming over the hill at any moment – most likely on foot – but so far they only have about sixty dollars and a nothing-special photo camera, far less than they probably expected to be able to grab quickly from us. Sixty dollars is two months' wages, but they want more, something to make this worthwhile.

They're not looking at me, and I'm trying not to look at the bag, trying not to think about the bag. Or the guilt.

The second guy yells *'BOTAS! BOTAS!,'* pointing at Doug's shoes. Then he sees my boots, which are tied tightly to the back of my bike, and they step quickly past him, waving their rifles at me. My hands are shaking so much that it takes me too long to untie them. They're getting anxious, and the first guy steps closer. The barrel of his gun is a few inches from my head and they're shouting louder and louder for me to *hurry*. I finally get the boots undone and give them to the first guy, who wrenches them out of my hands and shouts for us to go NOW. He shifts his rifle upwards in his right hand while his left hand holds my boots, and his finger comes down on the trigger and he fires a shot. Into the air.

We go.

We get away from two bandits with loaded weapons having lost only a camera, sixty dollars and a pair of boots. It seems impossible. Lucky.

We're riding down the dirt road and I still have $3,000 in my bag. I start to shake. I look around and realize that we haven't seen any garbage on the streets in Georgia because there is nothing to buy. Nothing to throw away. It would have been difficult for us to spend half of that sixty dollars in a week.

I can flick a switch and get light and heat. Whenever I want.

And I feel guilty that I hung on to the $3,000. We are not lucky. We are disgusting.

It is not a crapshoot.

~

The sixties and seventies are always described as wonderful times when revolutions occurred and when an incredible amount of creative headway was made. You hear about the now-great people who found each other in those times – Coppola, Lucas, Murch, Bush, Cheney, Rumsfeld (okay, maybe not great), Harrison, Carver, McGuane, Wolf, Chatham, McMurtry – and worked together in utopic conditions where money may have been the ultimate goal, way, way off, but where it didn't immediately matter beyond how it could ensure survival and support young families. People still drove shitty cars and shopped twice a year for clothes, no matter how rich they had become. What was more important was the *ideal* those people found they had in common with each other and were working toward. How insane the odds against them were, but how they went ahead and did it anyway.

The atmosphere seems ripe for another era of utopic rela- tionships: a wrongful war, a population with enough under their belts to risk some of it for the sake of morality, anger, a widening gap – the same conditions that led us through the sixties and its revolutions. There's so much to protest and we do, but only half-heartedly, and that half-heartedness seems to destroy any energy we have.

Perhaps it's because we have too much that we assume freedom and choice as rights, not privileges or aspirations. The seventies seemed to me to be a flush time, yes, but a time before we became spoiled, before we knew what flush was, and the cost of it. Flush in ideas and collaboration as well as wealth, and not nearly as much to spend it on as now. Flush in 2006 means something completely different. It means double incomes *and* living on credit.

I'm not of the sixties and seventies era. My consciousness bloomed with Trudeau signing Canada's constitution in 1982. I was thirteen then, and it was the moment that made me realize the impact, effort, ideal of a sort of utopia that was on paper, abstract with a vision toward the practical. It seems to me that since then, what generations learn in their formative years changes so quickly that there is nothing to hang on to *but* change. What we learn now becomes obsolete so fast that any connection with it is splintered almost immediately, and there is no actual craft to fall back on, to incorporate the change into. What we learn now lacks a mythology. Or, at least, the mythology has a Teflon-like quality.

Coppola, Lucas, Murch – they don't look flush now. They *are* – we know that – but they did it honestly and carry it as such. I don't like to make a caste system of deservedness, but I do believe in a hierarchy of truthfulness, sincerity and hard work. Twenty-five years from now, I can't imagine sitting in front of the television (or whatever sort of screen we'll have then) watching a documentary about my peers, who connected, in a time when the political and ideological chemistry was right, with some larger-than-life vision that meant more to them than their own lives, understanding how important it would be at the exact moment it was born. Risking life and reputation to do it, to be part of it. Show me these people.

These people will be the unseen and the unacknow-ledged – the Cubans, the Georgians, the migrant workers in the Western world, or perhaps just those who occupy rural spaces the world over. It'll be the ones who know what it is to have nothing and nothing to lose. People who *know* processes, how things actually work – those whose needs have an actual purpose beyond consumption and propping up the economy. It won't be those who have lost their memories, who don't know struggle, who have never felt a collective spirit that keeps everything going because that's all there is. 'The crooked unimproved roads,' wrote Blake, 'are the roads of genius.' In our shiny, sparkly cities, we tend to forget that most of the world's roads have never been paved. Or how to endure a bit of discomfort to travel down them.

When I experience realizations like this, I usually start to burn things or give them away – journals, notes, clothes, letters – anything that might be a part of the arrogance of privilege or luck or accident. But I fear letting *everything* go, fear having nothing to refer to (what *then*?). A friend's sister decided at the age of twenty-two that she was going to join the order of the Poor Clares and become a cloistered nun. I was at her 'farewell' barbecue, which was the last time she was likely to see any of her family again.

She was leaving for Italy the next day and had been required to give away everything she owned. Everything. The hardest things, she said, were photos, because what they meant to her was meant to her alone – the feeling, the memory each photo created in her would not be repeated in someone else. This loss of person was difficult for her. More difficult than going to buy the burlap with which to make her habit, more difficult than giving away her last piece of non-cloistered clothing. She would be able to write letters from the monastery, at least. (Those would be letters I wouldn't throw away.)

The visual artist Giovanni Anselmo said, 'I, the world, things, life – we are points of energy, and it is not as necessary to crystallize these points as it is to keep them open and alive.' I often imagine throwing everything away or deciding to enter a cloistered order as being the equivalent of deciding to know nothing of yourself and no one knowing anything of you. Not admitting that you know nothing, but making a conscious decision not to know, which is a pretty solid presumption. If you're going to take such a large step as becoming a nun or ridding yourself of all your possessions, the one thing you are very likely to have is a possession of the self. If only to give it up. That's where the conviction to make such decisions comes from.

What I'm aiming for in this crapshoot, or perhaps just what resonates with me, is essentially an idealization of places or events that have never been experienced. It's the

Portuguese notion of *saudade* that's simmering: the feeling of yearning for something impossible to regain because it never quite existed. It's not quite homesickness or pining for someone loved or once loved, but more a longing, the opposite of the Proustian sense of wistfulness. It's mostly a pleasant feeling, but it can often be too located in the present and future to be practical.

Cuba and its political idealism meshed with its constantly morphing reality; Georgia's ability to fully function – socially, philosophically, anthropologically – without any amenities, but with a value system that helped keep the consequences of that lack of amenities from being as dire as it would have in most other places on earth; the ability to be alone somewhere, without consequence or harm to others, without being seen or heard, but while straddling that line of camouflaging yourself (by being unobtrusive, by being quiet and respectful) so that you might be able to stand tall in a field of wild flowers when you're not actually there (the goal being to remind yourself of how little you mean, how very well the world functions without you, how inconsequential any contribution you make is, and the freedom that lies in that realization – a freedom that is more helpful than any deliberate action of ego); how useless worry is to the state of things, and yet how reassuringly human it is, just like ego (I worry because I care – this makes me a good person); the arrogance of being alive and wanting to affect the world – these are all elements of longing, part of my nostalgia for the near-impossible.

The nostalgia I'm talking about is not a nostalgia for a specific time. 'It takes just one awful second, I often think, and an entire epoch passes,' says Sebald of our changing times, which have a tradition of abandoning landscapes and rituals and being self-destructive. A friend told me once that everything he did was motivated by his desire to return to the safety he felt in his childhood. This is not what I mean. The places I like, that I keep going back to or that I seek out for some reason, are places that remind me (or that I suspect will remind me) of a state of things – of a certain innocence, perhaps, or more specifically of simplicity. Of an innocence of complication, say, a simplicity necessitated by a period of jadedness.

To be able to walk into a room and turn on a light, turn up the heat. Every time I flick a switch now, I think of that long, lonely stretch of road I was on, of those balaclavas and Kalashnikovs. I can't say for sure whether we almost died. I don't know if their intentions were to shoot us (I suspect not) – if so, they had plenty of opportunity to do so, or at least had plenty of opportunity to do worse than they did. Drag us into the bushes. Make us undress. Rape. Take everything. Leave us for dead. None of which they did. So to say we almost died seems dishonest, even though they had the means to do the deed. And in that vagueness, that murkiness, lies a sympathy, maybe even empathy, for their actions: I think they had every right to kill me (or at least rob me), that the entitlement I came from ought to be a crime. They should have the boots, the camera, the $3,000. Most Georgians were struggling to have the heat in their houses and apartments turned back on. The loss of two tourists' lives, or the money they were carrying, is minimal compared to what they have already endured.

But I can flick a switch.

⸻

You're in an airplane, say, crossing an ocean or chunk of land at 700 or 800 km/h. You look around you. You notice the pattern of the plastic on the backs of the chairs in front of you, the people sitting on either side of you. You crane to look up and down the aisle. The white noise drone of the plane muffles the conversations going on (eavesdropping takes too much effort): the scenery of this plane is identical to the last. But then, the purpose of it is merely to get you there fast while distracting you from the fact that you're seven miles above the earth's surface in a piece of machinery, the physics of which do not add up. It's not meant to be an engaging or encouraging observation. If you're lucky enough to have a window seat, you have to straighten your back, put your forehead against the small Plexiglas oval and look sideways or down in an unnatural, straining fashion to see what you're torpedoing over. If the weather's stormy enough, you may see streaks of waves on the ocean; if it's a day or two before harvest, you may see the swaths of solid colours of the flower fields as you fly over Holland – but only then; if it's clear below the jet in summer you'll see tongues of ice in the mountains of northern climes, ripples of sand dunes one hundred feet high belting around the earth's middle. You will not, even if there's a force-ten wind, see the blades of the 5,000 windmills in Tamil Nadu's wind farm turning, or see actual people moving about on the ground anywhere in the same way you can see a jetliner from the ground. You'll be too high for that, too far away. It can give you a view of things you can never fully comprehend on the ground, yes, but the bland experience of the plane is exacerbated in one's lack of ability to observe detail from it; it can only capture large-scale things in their exaggerated states.

Once you've landed, you leave the frenetic atmosphere of the airport behind you. You step onto a train. The seats are lower, you can see other people's faces, hear their conversations more clearly; you're at eye level with the landscape. There are, in fact, things that are higher than you now. Large trees umbrellaing over the tracks, monuments, houses, cliffs, mountains. The windows are wider, more graceful, less restrictive. Towns rush past, but you catch a glimpse of people, at least, perhaps even snag moments or situations: a group of men outside a bar, say, where someone starts to throw a punch, cut off by the building that moves between you and them; a woman by a table in a house by the tracks, lit by a candle, her head down – is she crying? Or reading? Thinking about an affair she once had? She's long gone by the time those possibilities enter your head. The train passes through the outskirts of the town – you flash by a dog standing on the sandy bank of the railbed, panting, looking toward the front of the train as if wondering where it came from. For a while there is nothing – only trees and fields – but you notice the heron at the edge of the estuary, making the long slow-motion step of herons into the water, beak down, concentrated on the hunt. Some children emerge from the woods, running toward the tracks, though it's not quite clear whether they're running toward the train or running away from something, their expressions irresolute. You wonder what's happening out of the windows on the other side of the train.

The train begins to slow, and you pass a barrier of houses, into a town that becomes more and more densely populated as you travel closer to its centre. The train stops. You get out. Find a place to stay. Jet lag has rendered it impossible for you to absorb any more.

The next morning you get up, have some breakfast, decide to rent a bicycle. You're tired, but you figure some exercise will push your body and mind past that. You get on the bike, and start pedalling.

~

Call me old-fashioned, but I like the texture of slowness. How it lacks invasiveness. The repertory theatre once a month instead of a DVD and on-demand television every night. The typewriter instead of email. Letterpress printing instead of digital typesetting. The train instead of the plane, the bicycle not the car. The Coleman lantern or candles instead of the energy-efficient halogen lamp. Slowness permits a capturing of moments, and even of glimpses of energy inherent to certain things – the energy Anselmo was talking about – which would be impossible with contemporary speed. I don't deny the efficiency or convenience of speed – sometimes it's essential or, at the very least, it comes in handy – but the cost of it is too much to bear most times, and so I usually hover around an ideal that views takeout and anything 'to go' as unappealing.

I'm under forty, so that tends to put me in the bracket of 'visionless Luddite,' not owning a cellphone and structuring my life so that things like a visit to the city become events (mostly because of the ferry and three-hour bike ride it involves) rather than presumptions, rights or entitlements. It's much easier to enjoy and appreciate events than those other things. I note with relief (and some glee) that in most European cities, it's difficult to find a place that will give you coffee in a paper or Styrofoam cup. You *must* sit and enjoy it on the premises – a sort of forced civility and refusal to bow to speed – and, oddly enough, one tends to enjoy it more while sitting down and taking in the surroundings, even when one is forced to.

I lived in Geneva for a short while and would run a few mornings each week to get the bugs out, and each morning the same man would lean out of his window and shout, '*Mon Dieu, mademoiselle! Prends un café et un croissant!*' I'm sure that if I'd knocked on his door he would have quickly set the table. Slowness is a way to something beyond privilege. It is a way to grace.

Living in North American cities has recently started to make me numb. I suspect it makes most people numb but, since you're numb, the consequences of that sensation go unrecognized until you realize you can't use a (or several) limb(s). This doesn't discount the vibrancy of North American cities, or the numbness you can feel in the backwaters of any place too far away from them, but my feeling is that we're putting disproportionate importance on urban culture and its speed and invasiveness (on the other hand, doing so leaves the rural areas deliciously empty) and the tendency to indulge in things simply because they're there or because we can, careering toward an all-out acknowledgement that we are, as Michael Ignatieff says, 'the only species with needs that exceed our grasp.' There's an attractiveness to that kind of ravenous thinking, but I don't know how deep it runs. When things run out, they run out. Slowness is more penetrating, but wilfully so, and in a kinder fashion. It's easier to grasp (and hang on to). There is time to replace what's being consumed, and to consider the significance of consumption. You're no longer cut off from the innate need to be self-sufficient, to experience a sort of basic survival. In cities, 'survival' and 'self-sufficiency' take on different meanings, and while cities do tend to release people from the constraints of physical work required in the traditional sense of the term (gathering food, wood for heat, etc.), they present their populations with other constraints, among which is a loss of certain connection related to that innate need. In the country, that innate need, and therefore the harmony, is based on a raw sort of nature and necessity. Cities are, it seems to me, designed to keep that nature at bay, and that denial has always slightly confused me. There's no denying the feeling of possibility in cities, but I suspect it's easy to feel because it's contained. If you stand in the prairie at the edge of Calgary looking east, away from the city, in all that big sky, the possibility you sense is vast – so vast that it seems impossible to capture, and it takes an increasingly rarefied person to grab onto it there, and not among the oil-baron skyscrapers popping out of the ground to the west. Limitation makes you appreciate opportunity.

Vastness makes you depressed at how it's being misused, or not used at all.

But back to the bike.

~

You get on the bike and you start pedalling. You pass from the centre of town to its outskirts, pass fountains, pass women towing carriages filled with vegetables from the market, carrot fronds protruding and bouncing with each of their steps. You pass children playing soccer in a park, a store that sells only typewriter ribbons, lovers entangled behind thickets, and you pass a fish shop that has its door open so that when you're alongside it, you pass through an invisible curtain of decaying sea smell that lingers longer than its approach did.

You pass side streets and in a fit of spontaneity take a sharp turn to the right onto one of them and enter into a cul-de-sac of seemingly identical houses. But as you ride in circles around them, you begin to see the human touches that distinguish them. Planters of geraniums in front of one, a rosehip bush in front of another. Magnolias in bloom on one street, on the next a mixture of horse chestnut and maple. There is no one on any of these streets, but these small details make them feel cared for, if not alive.

You find your way back to the main street, passing a butcher who is dumping unsaleable offal into a shallow bin behind his shop, surrounded by scrawny, yelping dogs, their tails wagging stiffly and high, fervently. You leave town on an *allée* fringed by sycamore trees and pass into

fields of flowering rape, carpets of yellow bordered by the
enthusiastic green that trees and bushes seem to have in
May. When you get tired, you turn down a small footpath
between two fields and sit under a banyan tree, the shift-
ing, dappled light that filters through its leaves hypnotiz-
ing you into sleep. Your dream is infused with the scent
of melons, the sound of wind in chest-high plants and the
occasional car passing.

You wake, not knowing whether you've slept or merely
dozed, not knowing what time it is, but knowing that it
doesn't matter. You wake in a different place than you fell
asleep in – it's the same place, of course, but you recog-
nize nothing in it from what you saw before. Your eyes
are drawn to the rocks in the dirt at your feet, the lone
insect crawling around a stream of milky sap on the bark
of the banyan. As you stare at it, you remember reading a
long time ago that the sap is sometimes used for polishing
copper and brass, and put on rashes and bruises to calm
the inner workings of the skin. That didn't seem important
at the time, but it could be useful now. You get up slowly,
stretch, feel the wind ripple through your shirt, touching
your skin. You stand for a moment, looking. Just looking.
And then you get on the bike and pedal back. You have a
meal that tastes like the hunger you have created, all the
smells and sensations of it amplified by your day's exertion.
You sleep soundly.

Jet lag has you up before dawn, so you go for a walk. It's that
time of day when it's both early and late. In the same block you
hear a drunken man arguing in circles with his friends, who
are trying to quiet him, and you see a woman standing in her

kitchen, rubbing one of her eyes as she pours some hot coffee from a silver canister. You walk through empty streets, mostly blind for the lack of daylight. You hear the exact moment when the songbirds start to sing, and it's not gentle, the way it is in the movies or when you lie between walls and behind windows and under a roof. It's almost deafening – terrifying and comforting at the same time, this non-human thing. The air is charged with electricity and when an errant, surprising bolt of lighting lights up the sky, you see in a split second the ditch you didn't know you were walking beside, and the large carp coursing through it, fin tearing up the surface of the still water. As the light quickly dissolves back into darkness, you make out the road, flat out ahead, disappearing into barriers of landscape. No rain follows, the air dry and crackly.

You walk and you walk and you can feel in your legs that you're walking uphill. It gets steeper and steeper and by the time the sun is up, you see that you're quite high above the valley floor, surrounded by brain-like hedges with paths weaving in and out of them. Up ahead, you spot a flash of colour in the hedges, there, again, and as you get closer you realize it's a person, a group of people, and they're wearing woven baskets on their backs that are supported by a strap across the forehead and they're picking the top leaves of the hedges that look like lush green brains and putting them into the basket. They look up and smile when they see you, and say something encouraging, all the while picking, and you stand there and you smell tea and you watch them and rest and then you wave and keep going. You walk along the road, higher and higher through three more plantations before you stop again.

There's a whoosh and you look up to see a hawk in an updraft, playing in the wind, not too far away from you, but farther than you would have expected from the loudness of the whoosh. There's a small town ahead and you start to walk again, past more colourful tea-pickers, making way for the small trucks that occasionally pass and that pick up the large burlap sacks of tea leaves left by the side of the road. The air smells fermented, full of the fragrant humidity of the plucked leaves. You know you will never forget it.

You walk into the town, which is very small, and someone sees you and smiles and pulls a chair out of her house, setting it in the shade under a tree that looks like a jacaranda but isn't. She tells you to sit and when you don't, because you don't know how to respond, she takes her small hand, loops her forefinger and thumb around your wrist and guides you to it. She brings you tea. It's orange. It's hot, steaming nectar with a wisp of citrus and tannin. She smiles when you smile. It brings tears to your eyes.

On the road, near the quiet store selling eight different kinds of bananas and freshly made yogurt from the milk of a local water buffalo, a man pounds something in a mortar. Some children are playing with a rock and a piece of string.

There is something about this place. You stay.

~

You realize how loosely defined your surroundings are now. You were strapped to the plane seat, strapped to the railway tracks and the road on which you biked. You've moved from the sterile to the more imaginative, informative.

On foot you're strapped merely to your feet. You need not follow the road, though it does occasionally make things easier. But that ease is like a set of tracks, difficult to derail oneself from. You remember the last time you were in the Rocky Mountains, a place you'd spent a good long while, though not in a few years. You were there in June, a time when the highway used to be void of tour buses, and you were shocked to find yourself counting fifty of them in one short stretch now. This depressed you until you mentioned it to a friend who pointed out the genius of keeping hundreds of thousands of tourists in a fragile national park bound to a stretch of asphalt thirty-feet wide – bound without them realizing it. All you have to do to get away from it is step off the road. You will be alone.

Your feet, though sore now, will take you just about anywhere. To. From. Through. Alongside. Over. Under. Around. Detour. If you let them. You were in northern Holland once, on some islands that were more difficult to reach than most other places in the country. It was a beautiful summer day in a month that was not-quite-summer, and the island was busy (though not as busy as it can get) with visitors. The island was famous for its enormous lengths (and widths) of beaches and the tides that would suddenly provide an extra two or three hundred feet of it. You walked along one that was completely deserted, thinking you must be far from the town where the ferry was, but when you looked up, away from the sand, away from the sea, at the fringes of the beach, you saw hordes of people.

Sitting, standing, drinking, eating, playing Frisbee. None of them on the beach. Shopping. Reading. Relaxing. You looked back at the sea, wondering if they knew something that you didn't, wondering if a rogue wave was about to come and sweep you away, or if there was a DO NOT TRESPASS sign that you missed. You, the only person on this area of sand so vast it had no end but the horizon. But no, it was just you, and all of them over there, straining against the invisible barrier between beach and not-beach, nearly spilling over it but staying with everyone else, contained in an imaginary box of safety that, being from a much larger country famed for its vastness, was lost on you. Holland was constantly complaining about its crowded conditions, and here was a perfect way to break away, but this self-invented, if not self-imposed problem of overcrowdedness kept them within it, afraid of space, or unsure of how to navigate it. You remember how funny it seemed at first, strictly as a display of subconscious human behaviour, then how disturbing. A friend had told you once about a famous picture in which the border collie of the Canadian embassy in Washington had successfully corralled a party of 500 people into the corner of a very large ballroom without anyone noticing, and this reminded you of that, only the border collie was supplanted by a certain kind of mentality that you'd always thought would naturally tend toward freedom and space, but that had disappointed you again and again. You remember Jim Harrison saying that our culture has shoved us into a consensual box from which most of us don't want to be liberated. You're not so smart when it comes to understanding mass thinking. You need him to explain it, to help you understand.

You sit in this small town for a few days, thinking about these things and watching what goes on around you. You think about the price of speed, and the price of slowness; a ubiquitous, gentrification of experience versus a lack of ability to absorb many things all at once and the subsequent perceived lack of vision. You think about the carp and the asphalt you saw in the flash of light, and you don't know what to make of any of it.

~

The tea you sip during the day is unbelievable. You'll never have tea at home again, at least not while the taste of this is in your memory. You'll never put anything in your mouth that has been in Styrofoam.

In the morning the old men come to the square in their sarongs, sit on the ground or the curb of the carless road and read the paper until they are done. Sometimes children bring them tea – five or six small glasses held in a wire rack so they can be carried without spilling, the precursor to the paper cup holder. The men must let the tea cool before they can put their fingers on the glass, bring the glass to their mouth, enjoy it in small sips, sugar cubes held between their teeth.

The children go to school. Occasionally, a woman walks down the street, filling a basket with things from each of the stores, stopping to talk to owners. The men with the newspapers are gone. At noon, when the tea-pickers have finished their eight-hour shift, the street becomes busy with people engaged in the daily commerce of life: waiting for a bus, buying a snack, making phone calls from the phone house, looking for nails.

And so on. You talk to those people, get to know them beyond their routines: the old man who buys eight rounds of bread every morning for his grandchildren's lunches, then returns in the afternoon for a small cone of freshly roasted peanuts; the woman who buys a mickey of arrack every day for her husband, even though she doesn't want to – he scares her when he drinks; the young girl who has told you her names for all the stray dogs and cats in town, who laughed when you asked if she would be a veterinarian one day. But there comes a day when you know you have to leave, that spending life just sitting is a sort of luxury, but also knowing that making the decision to sit for a while, surprising yourself and your societal wiring toward speed and progress, will affect how you do things from now on. How you see things. You'll sit, do nothing, observe more often, even though you know it may not always bring good. You might sit in the courtyard of the Hyatt in Atlanta like your father did, where all the hotel rooms have balconies cheerfully jutting out into it, and you'll probably look up when you hear a strange whistling noise and you see a man falling and you'll start to stand up, but before you're fully straightened, he'll have hit the ground beside you. Blue. You won't see this while craning your neck unnaturally to look out the plane window, or from the train rushing through the suburbs. You might

catch a glimpse of something falling if you're bicycling by, you might hear the thud, the quick silence, then the cry of witnesses if you're walking past, but you'll experience nothing of that particular movement if you're not sitting still. When you sit still, things have a tendency to become less about you.

You'll sit outside the Louvre for a few days, absorbing, before going in to absorb more, better. You'll go to the airport, not to leave, but to stand at the departure and arrival gates just watching because you want to understand the anguish that seems easy to display at an airport, the anguish of knowing the distance that will separate, the realization of a promise broken, or the bliss (or a change of heart) upon seeing someone again. To see the collision between waiting and the force of the philosophy of speed, of the plane. All that waiting, only to get somewhere faster. And all that speed, only to arrive somewhere – Toronto, Janice, twin daughters who have grown so much in the week you were away – that is or is not home.

My *saudade* is such a specific state of simplicity that I'm afraid to write it down, to explain it fully, because defining it exactly may cause it to disintegrate. I'm happy to have it hover around me in a vague state despite how occasionally and temporarily destructive it can make me. To be a little less than vague, however, for purposes of illustration, I know it involves silence. Not a total silence, but the kind of silence that brings one into hearing again. The kind of silence we had in the one-room, electricity- and plumbing-free, woodstove-heated cabin, which sets the ears ringing at first, then dissolves into the noise of the world just being. Wind. Raindrops. Birds. The hollow bark of a dog over the next hill, a mile away. One lonely car swishing by on the highway below. The hum of very few things.

My *saudade* involves invisibility, which is a conflicted desire in that its intention is humble but it has a selfish means. I spend my whole life trying not to be seen, which has the effect of turning me inwards into myself, though I'm doing it because I despise selfishness and arrogance and want to rid myself of it. Regardless, this invisibility I crave is of the kind of standing in the field that I described before.

It also involves time and space for contemplation, though this is perhaps something that is a natural product of silence and invisibility. My *saudade* has no one image of physical geography or place that will provide all of those things I want and need (there's that arrogance of fusion with humble intentions), but is a composite of a number of places where I've experienced significant moments of realization – the mountains of Georgia, the vast blue sierras of Mexico, the tea stations of Sri Lanka – all steep and difficult landscapes, but then, says Harrison, we survive by learning from pain and we learn what we need by suffering. I suspect the one I'll settle on in my imagination (since, by definition, I'll never have it) will be in Canada because it is home, and settling on a *saudade* that exists in a place where one has no innate rights feels obtrusive to me, and counter to the whole personal philosophy that it must not affect anyone else. (Beyond that, home is just home and that's what makes it home.) In Amsterdam, the sound of a motorboat on a canal is a comfort (to my *saudade*) because it's the same noise that I woke up to while living on the Rideau Canal. They're both places I love, and the comfort is not the noise itself, but knowing that it is possible to exist, and for *saudade* to exist, in a multitude of landscapes.

And how is this selfish, arrogant longing helpful in the grand scheme of things? I'm not sure it's any more helpful than invading countries with ulterior motives or continually redecorating one's house to keep up one's status, but those sorts of things can be explained away and this can't. It's the unexplainable and indefinable and mysterious, like *saudade* itself, that we need to take stock of if we're going to survive with any sort of curiosity or interest in our condition.

Harrison's assertion that we have to look at this world from the inside toward the outside, and not the reverse, is a convenient justifier of such an isolationist *saudade*, but I've always felt that there's more to be deeply learned from minimalism than from overexertion of the senses.

This minimalism doesn't discount a variety of experiences – rather it streamlines the experiences, cuts to the chase, which is important for someone who can easily get lost in the intensity of so many things. It eases the guilt I feel from entitlement, because it is enough, not too much. It's a way of refusing to subscribe to it.

It is a kind of future.

# Acknowledgements

All photos were taken by the author, with exceptions cited below.

**LETTER TO A FRIEND (WHOSE MOTHER IS DYING)**
The map was taken from the *Insight Map of Sri Lanka* (Fürstenfeldbruck: Berndtson and Berndtson oHG, 1999).

**ESPERO**
'Espero' was previously published in the anthology *Habaneras* (Pasdeloup Press, 2004). The map was taken from the Santiago de Cuba portion of the Joint Operations Graphic (AIR), Series 1501 AIR, Sheet NF18-14 (U.S. National Imagery and Mapping Agency, edition 5, 1996).

**RAINY SUMMIT**
The photo of Liselotte Geue on p. 54 was taken by Elke Mack. The map is a detail from 'Railways – B.C. and Yukon 1904,' printed in the first edition of the *Atlas of Canada* (Department of the Interior, 1906).

**SQUEEZING A SPIRAL INTO A SQUARE HOLE**
'Squeezing a Spiral into a Square Hole' appeared
in the Summer 2006 issue of *Brick* magazine. All
quotes by Robert Bringhurst were taken from *The
Elements of Typographic Style*, version 2.4 (Hartley
and Marks, Publishers, 2001). The coasters and
compass are by Walter van Broekhuizen. The map
was taken from 'architectuurkaart amsterdam' (ARCAM
Architectuurcentrum Amsterdam, 2005).

**LIKE LANDSCAPE DIDN'T MATTER**
The quote on p. 75 about ring roads is taken from John
Hanson Mitchell's *Walking Towards Walden* (Addison-
Wesley, 1995). The quotes from Simon Schama on pp. 81,
82 and 94 were taken from the introduction to *Landscape
and Memory* (Alfred A. Knopf, 1995). Jim Harrison's
quote on p. 82 was found in *Returning to Earth* (Grove
Press, 2006). Peter Taylor's comment about identity on
p. 86 was taken from his short story 'The Old Forest,'
published in *The Granta Book of the American Long
Story* (Granta Books, 1998). The photo on p. 89 was
taken by Walter van Broekhuizen. The map was taken
from the 'Topografische Fietskaart Amsterdam Noord-
Holland zuid' (Algemene Nederlandsche Wielrijders-
Bond, 2005).

**THE END OF THE DIRT ROAD ON A DETOUR TO DARWIN**
David Mitchell's quote on p. 104 appeared in his novel
*number9dream* (Sceptre, 2001). The map is a detail
from the 'Commonwealth of Australia,' published in

the *Official Year Book of the Commonwealth of Australia*, (Melbourne: McCarron, Bird and Co., 1916).

**SYMBOLS OF INFINITY**
'Symbols of Infinity' was excerpted in the *National Post* on February 21, 2004, and appeared in whole in *Outpost* magazine's March/April 2004 issue. The map is a detail from 'NWT Explorers' map published by the Department of Natural Resources.

**BORDERLAND**
'Borderland' appeared in the summer 2004 issue of *Geist* magazine. The map is a detail taken from the 'Railways – Manitoba, Saskatchewan and Alberta, 1904,' printed in the the first edition of the *Atlas of Canada* (Department of the Interior, 1906).

**∞**
'∞' was shortlisted for *PRISM International*'s literary non-fiction award for 2005. The photo on p. 135 was taken by Yevgeni Khaldei (©Yevgeni Khaldei/Corbis). Bruce McCall's mock application for immigration to Canada, quoted on pp. 132 and 145, appeared in the *New Yorker*'s November 22, 2004, issue. The W. G. Sebald poem on p. 137 was published in *Unrecounted* (Hamish Hamilton, 2004). Vaclav Havel's quote on p. 144 appeared in his essay 'The Power of the Powerless,' published in *Open Letters: Selected Writings, 1965–1990*, ed. Paul Wilson (Vintage Books, 1992). The quote on American contemporary culture on p. 145 was taken

from Jeff Sharlett's essay 'How Clear Channel Programs America,' which appeared in the December 2003 issue of *Harper's* magazine. The map is a detail from the 'Railways – B.C. and Yukon 1904,' printed in the first edition of the *Atlas of Canada* (Department of the Interior, 1906).

**SAUDADE**

The quotes on pp. 155 and 177 attributed to Michael Ignatieff were taken from *The Needs of Strangers* (Picador, 2001). The Jim Harrison quote on fate on p. 163 was found in *Off to the Side* (Grove Press, 2002). William Blake's quote on p. 169 appeared in *The Marriage of Heaven and Hell, 1790-1793*. The comment by Giovanni Anselmo on p. 170 was taken from literature accompanying the 'Zero to Infinity: Arte Povera' exhibition which appeared at the Walker Art Center in Minneapolis between October 2001 and January 2002. W. G. Sebald's comment on the passing of time on pp. 171-172 was taken from *The Rings of Saturn* (Vintage, 2002). The Jim Harrison quote on culture on p. 183 was found in *The Summer He Didn't Die* (Grove Press, 2006), and his comment on p. 188 on how to look at the world appeared in *Off to the Side*. The photo on p. 164 was taken by Doug Sage. The photo of the courtyard of the Hyatt Hotel in Atlanta on p. 186 is of unknown provenance, discovered on a found postcard. The map is a detail from 'Railways – Ontario and Quebec, 1904,' printed in the first edition of the *Atlas of Canada* (Department of the Interior, 1906).

## Acknowledgements

The cover image is taken from a tactical pilot chart of Abkhazia issued by the Defense Mapping Agency, 1992. The author photo was taken by Walter van Broekhuizen.

The Canada Council for the Arts provided subsistence funding for *Saudade*, for which I am extremely grateful. This book could not have been written without the help and support of my entire family, and my closest friends, including Delphine Courtillot, Theresa Kishkan, John Pass and Chris Koentges. Finally, this book encompasses all of the aspects of my life – past, present and future – which I see every day in my mother, father and sister, and in Walter, and in Laszlo. Thank you for everything.

ANIK SEE is the author of *A Fork in the Road* (MacMillan, 2000). Her writing has appeared in *Brick, Prairie Fire, Fiddlehead, Geist, grain,* the *National Post, Toronto Life* and, as a contributing editor, in *Outpost* magazine. She divides her time between Canada and Holland, where she works with books, old and new. Her new short story collection will be published by Freehand Books in 2009.

# Colophon

Typeset in Garamond
Printed and bound at
the Coach House on bpNichol Lane,
September 2008

Edited by Christina Palassio
Designed by Anik See

Coach House Books
401 Huron St. rear
on bpNichol Lane
Toronto, ON M5S 2G5
Canada
416 979 2217
mail@chbooks.com
www.chbooks.com